ISBN 978-0-364-73497-1
PIBN 11074878

CONTENTS.

I. FRANCE, its Growth and Consolidation,
By E: A: Freeman.
II. The countess of ALBANY, CHARLES EDWARD and ALFIERI, By A. Hayward, Q. C.
III. The VENETIAN INQUISITION, By T: A. Trollope.
IV. HERDER, GOETHE, and CARL-AUGUST,
By K: Hillebrand.
V. CLEOPATRA.
VI. Puritan and Cromwellian ENGLAND,
By J: R: Seeley, etc.
VII. MOLTKE, By Himself.
VIII. Princess DASHKOV.
IX. SCANDERBEG.
X. ZINZENDORF and the MORAVIANS.
XI. Gen. KALB.
XII. COLUMBUS.
XIII. The Greatness of the ROMANS, By Goldwin Smith.
XIV. The IRON MASK.
XV. The PRISONER of CHILLON.
XVI. DANTE, By M. Creighton.
XVII. ERASMUS.
XVIII. The GERMAN Reformation, By K: Blind.
XIX. Pocahontas, By H: Adams.
XX. FOUQUET the Magnificent, By F: W. Shelton.
XXI. The ASSASSINS.
XXII. BONAPARTE'S Political Position, By J: R: Seeley.
XXIII. POLISH HISTORY.
XXIV. The British in INDIA, By E. L. Godkin.
XXV. The legend of FRIEDRICH Barbarossa,
By Bayard Taylor.
XXVI. CALVIN and Servetus, By L. W. Bacon.
XXVII. Captain Kidd, By E: Everett Hale.

INDEX.

NOTE.—The Roman numeral preceeding the Arabic indicates the number of series, Small capitals the title of an article, Spaced type, the author.]

Adams, H: XIX.

Albania, mediæval history, IX, 1.

ALBANY, COUNTESS OF: ignorance of, why should be remembered, II, 1; family, birth, becomes canoness, 6; is married, character, 7; appearance, 10; leaves her husband, 12; goes to Rome, 13; arrangement with husband, goes to Colmar, 15; grief at husband's death, 16; does not marry Alfieri, visits England, presented at court, 17; gets a pension, leaves Paris for Florence, 18; society at Florence, summoned to Paris, death, will, 20.

Alfieri: birth, education, II, 8; love affairs, 9; meets countess of Albany, 10; her influence, 11; in Florence, 11, 18; manner of writing, 12; in Rome, 13; love for horses, 14; goes to England, 15; dies, will, 19.

America, discovery of, XII.

America, United States of: foundation of Va., XIX, 2-8; [see SMITH, KIDD] revolutionary war, XI, 3.

Antonius, character, V, 4.

ASSASSINS, the, power of their chief, devotion to him, how explained, XXI, 1; description of their "paradise," 2-3; origin of name "assissin," 6; later history of order, 7-8.

Bacon, L. W., XXVI.

Blind, K. XVIII.

Bodenstedt, OI.

BONAPARTE'S power springs not from the revolution, but from war, XXII, 1; his success due less to popular lassitude than to importance of army, 2; its necessity the foundation of this, hence the impossibility of peace, 3, 7; his liberalism, 4; his conquests have precedent in partition of Poland, 5; his system existed before him, 6; his breadth of mind, 8; his heroism humbug, the vastness of his plans, his model not Carl, but Alexander, 8.

BONIVARD, F., misrepresented by Byron, a Catholic sinecurist, birth, opposes duke of Savoie, XV, 2; loses benefice, imprisoned, not a martyr, release, 3; loose life, books, character, 4.

Calvin, dishonest treatment of Servetus, XXVI, 1-4;—ism, decline of, VI, 4.

Carl August, character, IV, 22; claims on country's gratitude, 23; "parsimony," 25.

Carlyle, his teaching and influence, VI, 7, 8.

Character, definition of, XX, 4.

Charles I, character, VI, 4; the Great, I, 6.

Chillon, prisoner of, see Bonivard.

CLEOPATRA, political character, relations with Cæsar, V, 1, 2; loves Antonius, efforts to keep her throne, cause of hatred felt for her by the Romans, not profligate according to ideas of time, 2.

COLUMBUS, youth in Lisbon, marriage, XII, 1, grand idea, 1, 2; ambition, 2, 3, 8, debts; in Spain, 2; demands conceded, 3; their nature, impossibility of realization, 4, 8; reaches West Indies, 4; selfishness, second expedition, disappointmens, 5; failure of his government, imprisoned, 6; last voyage, poverty, 7; death, character, 8.

Creighton, M., XVI.

Cromwell, VI, 2; character, 5, 9, 10; defective statesmanship, 6.

DANTE, birth, XVI, 1; meets Beatrice, inspired by her, 2; works, 3, 4; Beat-

THE

Q. P. INDEX ANNUAL

FOR

1881.

AN INDEX TO THE

ERNATIONAL REVIEW, THE POPULAR SCIENCE,

THE CENTURY, LIPPINCOTT'S, THE NATION,

THE ATLANTIC, THE LIVING AGE,

HARPERS, AND THE ECLECTIC,

FOR 1880-81.

THE Q. P. INDEXES NOW READY: Nation, $2.50; Atlantic, (sup.) $1.25; International, $1.00; Lippincott's, $2.00; Eclectic and Living Age, $3.00; Scribner's, $2.00; Annual, $100. IN PREPARATION, Index to the N. A. Review, 1861-1881.

"They are simply invaluable."—*T. W. Higginson.*

"Such indexes are just what I want."—*H. A. Tenney, State of Michigan Librarian.*

"Brief as it ("Lippincott" Index) is, I am very much pleased with it, and I have an opportunity of comparing it, perhaps, with the best work that is done."—*John Eaton, Commissoner of Education.*

"Enclosed find check for your capital help to learning."—*R. A. Guild, Librarian Brown Univ.*

"The indexes which I have received from you have saved me more time and labor than can be imagined. I would not be without them at any price." *M. A. Sanders, Pawucket Public Library.*

"Certainly, until some machine is devised by which a volume that we want springs from the shelf and takes its place by our side, opened at the desired page, we can hardly ask for more than this."—*Atlantic Monthly,* Feb. 1888

FREE PUBLIC LIBRARY, Worcester, Mass., March 2d. 1881. Dear Sir: I wish to say to you that I feel very much obliged to you for the indexes you are publishing. We find them very useful in this library, where we have to use megazines and reviews constantly in providing information needed in answering questions. *They are a library aid which it has been hard to get along without.* It is pleasant to learn that POOLE'S INDEX will be published in a year or so. I do not anticipate, however, that your indexes will be superseded by this publication. POOLE'S INDEX will be indispensable to large libraries and useful in all. *But, even in large libraries, indexes will still be needed that refer in greater detail to the contents of particular periodicals* than is possible in a work which indexes in a single, although large, volume a large number of magazines and reviews.

Poole's work will be useful in small libraries in enabling students to find out in what periodicals information is to be found, even although the libraries cannot themselves furnish the books. *Still, for smaller libraries, a few indexes, with many references, to sets of periodicals in their possession or taken by citizens of towns where they are situated,* MUST BE MUCH MORE USEFUL than one volume which makes comparatively scanty references to a great number of magazines and reviews, most of them not readily accessible to inquirers. Your indexes may be compared in this respect to the admirable INDEX TO HARPER'S MAGAZINE, which, on account of its fulness, will still be in constant use after Mr. Poole has got out his general index.

The appearance of this latter work I am awaiting anxiously, but, when it comes out, I expect to put it by the side of yours and to profit largely from the labors of both indexers. Very truly yours. Samuel S. Green, Librarian.

THE Q. P. INDEX ANNUAL, 1881.

This is an index to The INTERNATIONAL REVIEW, The POPULAR SCIENCE,* The CENTURY, LIPPINCOTT'S, The NATION, The ATLANTIC, HARPER'S, The ECLECTIC, and The LIVING AGE, for 1880-81.†

In this Index, the figures on the left of the decimal point indicate the volume; those to the right, the page; Roman numerals, the number of articles on the same subject. Names of persons in small capitals indicate that references are to articles by them;—in italics, that they are treated in their professional capacity. The letter w indcates that the figures following refer to reveiws of works on the subject indexed; *w*, to reviews of works by him; a, that the reference is to an article of considerable length. A* signifies that the work to which reference is made is illustrated; §, that it is travel; †, that it is poetry; ‡, that it is fiction; ¶, that it is a translation; ||, that it is history or biografy; **, letters or autobiografy; ††, art; ‡‡, religion; §§, the stage; ***, anecdote or incident.

Abdul Aziz, murder 33.3
About, 31.383
Abyssinia, hist 33.85
Académie française 33.465
Accomplishments, 18.496
Acquaducts, ps 11.26a: anc. 32.147a
Acta Comparationis 32.299
Adam, gov. 150.292a
Adams, C: F. 2d. q. 32.258, 294; *H. B.* 33.375: *J. Q.* 10.97**a; S: 33.431
Addison 33.418: *w* 32.157; 97.616; 151.73
Address, forms 13.292a
Adirondacks, 62.865a*; 63.-678a*
Ærostation 33.227
Æstheticism 33.28; temperament 48.139; evolution, 18-339a
Afganistan, hist. 31.247, 299; 32.161, 215, 274a; 33.45, 83, 85, 167, 168a, 187, 209, 242, 245, 327; 61.203
Africa, expl. 33.53; (central) 33.213, 156a; (N.) 32.318; 151.509; (S) 33.439
Agnosticism, 15.487a; 19.266; 149.719‡a; w 31.255‡
Air [see Ventilation] ground, ps 11.280a¶
Airlie, earl 33.245
Akominatos, 151.687a
Alaska, w 61.315
Albania, hist. 33.387
Albany, N. Y., hist. w 62.-524a*;
Albany, "count," 150.192; duke 33.407
Albertis 32.223
Alden, W. L. 33.456
Aldrich, T: B 62.390*
Alexander II, 32.275a; murder, 10.594a; 32.177, 271
Alfieri 47.61
Algebra, w 33.236a
Algeria, w 31.258; hist. 33.-167
Alhambra 27.425a*

*With this jourunal, only the less technically scientific articles have been indexed, but, as there is no general index to this periodical, we have added references to the volumes for several years past.

Figures to the left of the period indicate the vol. as follows: 10-11, Int. Rev.; 12-20, Pop. Sci.; 23, Century; 27-8, Lip.; 31-3, Nation; 47-8, Atl; 62-4, Harper; 97, Eclectic; 149.51, Living Age.

Alleghanies, trav 61.ii*
Allen, G. 47.371a; *J. H:* 32.267‖; W. 32.141; q 32.67, 90, 110; *W: F.* 31.336; 33.-393, 492
Allston, W 47.292*⁎*
Amenities of Home 33.158
America, archæ. ps 10.582a; 15.488a; 33.8; 63.670a; w 32.74; copper, 19.601; pottery, ps 11.573a*, discovery, 64.111a; w 33.196
America, Central, archæ 23.-228a*
America, U. S. of [see Middle States, Pacific, etc] area, 33.415; *administration* [see Civil Service, Weather-Bureau] agric, 31.373a; coast, 33.406; diplomatic (cost of change) 31.426: (consuls) 33.152a; Tresury, 33.323, 6; *agriculture* [see Breadstuffs, etc.] 33.414a; *climate* and character, 20.109a *constitution* (G: T. Curtis) 61.-101a: elections (Congress) 32.42; (pres.) 32.370; [vote] 31.420, 451; 32.83; pres. inability 33.113, 183, 188a, 206, 461; senate, 31.-385; *crime* [see Courts] homicide, w 31.465a; *education* [see Schools, Univ.] national aid, 31.433; decline of culture 32.88, 405; *finance* [see Banks, Silver, Tarif, Taxation] 31.-346, 299, 333, 453; 32.1, 22a; 33.21, 125, 163, 262, 363, 366; bonds 31.281, 401, 402; 32.35, 51, 84, 121, 141, 159, 251, 269, 341, 360; 33.284, 304, 386, 406; (registered) 33.75a; currency, 33.466a; (coin) 33.266a; (paper) 31.304, 451; det, 33.186, 389a, 444; (cities) 33.154; govt. & money-market, 33.287a; revenue, 33.106, 264, 442; stock fluctuations, 33.86a; nat. welth, 61.918a; *flag*, w 31.446; *forein relations* [see Infernal-machines] 32.-4; China, 31.453; 32.35, 42, 58, 70a; Egypt, Monroe d. in, 33.195; England [see Fortune Bay] 31.421; French claims, 33.326, 406; Spain, claims, 32.289; *history*, w 33.154¶, 381; early, w 32.-373; landing "pilgrims" 4.8-612a, 847;—1705-10, 11.-467a; revolution, 28.462*⁎*-a; 151.441;—1780, 33.435; (Loyalists' refuge) 27.391a; —1848-9, 11.97a;—1849-50; 47.234a; civil war, w 31.-341; 32.32; 33.10a, '200a, 216, 398a; 48.405; (abroad) 11.517a; elec. 1876 comp. with 80, 32.103; cont., 27.-517, 28.102; 47.103a; *immigration* 11.88a; 33.304; 150.350; German, 31.459; *industry*, influence Eur. ind. 11.580a; *pauperism*, 47.749a; *politics* [see Caucus, Civil-service, Democratic party, etc.] 31.352; 61.470; 62.307, 943; attentats, 33.32a; bribery, 31.356, 408, 425; 32.122; cabinet, 31.372a; [in Con.] 32.83, 107a, 110, 149; coalitions, 32.239; congress 33.406; [H. of R. apportionment] 32.20, 59a; 32.83; [speakership] 33.428, 447a; election

Figures to the left of the period indicate the vol. as follows: 10-11, Int. Rev.; 12.20, Pop. Sci.; 23, Century; 27-8, Lip.; 31-3, Nation; 47-8, Atl.; 62.4, Harper; 97, Eclectic; 149-51, Living Age.

expenses 33.389; executive, 28.610; 31.425; great men, 32.71a, 91, 110, 129a, 149, 218, 240; independents, 32.111a, 124a, 129, 148; "internal improvements" 32.123; canvas lies, 31.349, 385, 392, 442, 461; money, 31.338; nominations, preventing 32.166; reform, 33.74; "spoils" 33.388; "stalwarts," 33.94, 168; vice-president, 23.144; 33.61; *population*, 11.32a; 32.243, 278, 317, 352, 406; 33.394; forein, 32.168; [German] 33.135; *press*, 27.175a; 32.372; w 33.472; hoaxes, 33.149a;—German, 33.275,376; relig. 32.36, 74; *public law* [see Extradition] naturalization, 11.197a; 31.265; *society* 27.205*,*; w 63.627‡; abroad, 28.410a; caste, 48.823a; self-made man of culture 32.384a; 4th July, 61.634; news, 33.109; pesants, 27.161a; public spirit 23.145; reformers, 27.601a: servants, 27.520; stage Am. 32.146; titles 32.244; yung men 33.288a

American literature, 97.17a; abroad, 31.327, 359;—Boston, 62.381a*; —canvas songs, 31.284; filosofy, 47.443

"American" 32.277

Americanists 33.245

Amherst col. 17.120, 405; 33.493

Amicis 28.526; 32.170; 33.397; 48.833

Ammonia engine 32.318

Amos, S 32.100

Amusements, [see N. Y. etc] music & lit. club, 47.298

Anæstheties, w 33.354

Anam 33.25

Ancient history, w 33.123

Ancon, 32.136, 205

Ancona, A. d' 32.133

Andersen, H. C. 10.153

Anderson, J. 33.18; *M.* 31.446

Andover, hist. w 32.137

Andre, C 33.335

Andrew, J: A. w 33.77

Andrews bros. 32.66

Animals 33.254*,* secretiveness, 28.172a*; wild 28.473a*; legal persecutions, 17.619a

Ann, cape 23.49a*

Annapolis acad, 33.285

Anne, queen, son 151.443a

Année artistique 33.50

Anti-Monopoly league, 32.160, 199, 203a, 33.143, 146, 166, 265

Antinopoulos q. 31.255

Anthropology, 13.668a; 16.124a

Ants, 28.79a; 150.176a; 151.320

Antwerp museum, 33.174

Apes, 13.431a*

Arabs, 150.186¶

Arago, 16.114

Aratus 31.261¶

Arbitration, int. 33.144

Archæology, w 33.437; Am. institute, 32.12, 94, 403a; 33.8, 413; 61.797; frauds, 13.197

Architecture, church, Ital. w 31.345; house, Eng. 62.481a*

Arctic expl. w 33.420; Nor-

Figures to the left of the period indicate the vol. as follows: 10-11, Int. Rev.; 12-20 Pop Sci.; 23, Century; 27-8, Lip.; 31-3, Nation; 478, Atl.; 62-4, Harper; 97, Eclectic; 149-51, Living age.

wegian, 33.276, 435; U. S. 15.557; 32.304; 33.208, 245, 264, 326, 346
Ardennes, 28.539a*
Argyll, duke of. 33.262
Arithmetic, 16.206a; notation, 13.420a
Arkansas, pronunciation, 32.351
Armenia, 33.30, 187
Army, U. S., 33.366 drunkenness, 32.149, 240, 32.-296; rations, 32.243; sickness, 33.386;—and navy, 61.118a
Arnold, B 32.352; E. 64.-31*; *w* 31.312†; 47.428; M. q 31.398
Arnoth, N ps 10.100*
Aronson 31.274
Arran islands 62.506a*
Art [see Pictures] w 32.186; 33.9a; *artists'* personality 150.149a; *exhibitions*, N. Y. 27.417; 32 80a, 229, 250, 285, 335; 48.193a; 63.143; *journals*, 27.312; 48.715; *museums*, 27.208; N. Y., 32.335;—*ancient*, w 32.-279; Dutch, 61.52a*, 845a*; 63.177a*; Ital. 150.149a; popular, 28.418; relig. 62.-321a*; —originality, 18.-697; monstrous, 14.781a
"Art, l'" 32.120; 33.35; "Review," 33.333
Arthur, C. A. 31.245; 32.359, 397; 33.4, 21, 22, 148, 226, 242, 244, 247, 261, 323; q 32.122
Aryans, 47.224a, 478a
Asfalt, 19.539a
Asia, central, Russians in, 32.181a; 33.129
Assassins 63.440
Assos 32.12
Assyriology, 32.300a, 353, 405
Astor, W. W. 33.323, 392
Astronomy, w 33.76, 416; cont. 33.94; almanacs, 32.-12; music sferes, 63.286;—Soc. medals, 32.261
Athene statue 32.92
Athens, 62.819a* mediæval, 151.685a; archæ school, 32.403a
Athletics, 16.677a; 19.7a
Atkinson, E: q 31.316; *w* 11.339a; 32.132
Atlanta exhib. 33.197, 245, 284, 366, 386, 426, 485
Atlantic coast, U. S. 61.835; steamer routes, 23.91a; tel. 33.65, 485
Atlantis, 15.759a
Atlases, 31.411; 33.472; hist. 33.274
Atmosfere, "transfig." 32.186
Aubrey, mrs 47.433
Aucassin & Nicolette, 27.-216
Audubon, 31.341; 61.665a*
Auerbach 47.577
"Auf der Höhe" 33.434
Austen, J.. 62.308.
Australia, bush life, 10.87a; soc. 32.44; tarifs, 33.243; aborigines, 19.680a*
Austria, fi. 33.387; forein rel. 33.325; hist., cont. 32.-232
Autograf col. 86.383
Auton, C 33.498
Autumn 61.857a*
Ayres, A 32.157.
B*abcock, E. W* 33.361
Babies, ps 10.39a 17.629a; food, 19.598a, language, 13.587a; 14.591a

Figures to the left of the period indicate the vol. as follows: 10.11, Int. Rev.; 12-20, Pop. Sci.; 23, Century; 27.8, Lip.; 31.3, Nation; 47-8, Atl.; 62.4, Harper; 97, Eclectic; 149-51, Living Age.

Bacon, F 97.611; 151.69; L. 33.513
Bagehot, ps 11.110
Bailey, S. M 33.205
Bain, A 32.243
Baird, S. F. 62.549*
Baker pasha 63.786; C A 33.-387; *W: M.* 33.98
Bakunin 33.119
Baldwin, J. 32.340
Balfour, F. M. 33.221
Baltimore, P. ly. 33.221, 112
Balzac, 32.114
Bamford, S. 149.750
Bandelier, A. F. 32.94; 33.-8; 63.793
Bangor collectorship, 33.2, 103
Bankers Asso., 33.128
Bankrupt law, U. S. 32.464; 33.104, 126, 326
Banks, nat. 11.297a; 33.126, 304, 484; and govt. 32.144; mismanagement, 33.403: supervision 33.441; taxation, 33.226, savings, 12.-239
Baptism, w 33.238a
Baptists, 7th day, 23.214a
Bar Asso., N. Y. 33.245; U. S. 33.146
Baragiola, 33.474
Barbauld, mrs. 151.579a
Barbizon, 23.268
Barbou, A. 32.249¶; 63.313
Bardeen, C. W. 33.115
Barine, A., q 33.255
Baring-Gould, 32.414
Barker, G: F. 15.693a* W. 32.326; q 33.247
Barlow. G. 33.14†
Barnard, F. A. P. ps 11.100*
Barrett, L. 33.298
Barth, A. 33.435
Bartholdi, statue 33.327
Bartlett, J: 33.331: W: F. 31.305; W. O. 33.245
Bastian, A. 32.280; *H. C.* 61.953
Bathybius, ps 11.641a¶
Bats, 28.236a*
Bavaria, hist. 33.407
Bayard, J. 31.245; 32.92: 33.-284; q 31.433
Baynes, T. S. q 33.115
Beaconsfield, 27.624; 32.270, 327, 331a; 33.278a, 459; 63.-308; 97.1a, 143; 150.29a; *w* 31.413a: 47.445, 715‡; 62.466; 150.55a
BEARD, W. H. 62.i**; *G. M.* 33.100; 63.631
Beauty, nat. appreciation of 147.192; personal 33.292a
Beck, 33.445
Becker B. H. 32.188
Bedford park, 62.481a
Bee culture, 61.777a
Beecher, T: K. 31.357
Beer-drinking, 48.573, 855
Beeseau, 32.340
Beissel, C. 23.216a
Belgium, schools, 32.279
Belgioso, 48.644
Belgrade, 88.255
Beljame, A. 33.416
Bells, Burma, 150.502
Belot, A 32.227¶
Benedict, J. 33.139
Benevolence, 13.735a
Benfey, T. 33.117: *w* 32.133; ly. 33.354
Benjamin, S. G. W. 32.-193
Benton, J. G. 33.167
Bernard, C 13.742*
Bergen, 47.770a, *T. G.* 33.-354
Bergstrom, 33.153
Berkeley, 33.19

Figures to the left of the period indicate the vol. as follows: 10-11, Int. Rev.; 12-20, Pop. Sci.; 23, Century; 27-8, Lip.; 31-3, Nation; 47-8, Atl.; 62-4, Harper; 97, Eclectic; 149-51, Living Age.

Berlioz, 48.746a; 97.531a; 150.478a; *w* 32.13; 62.806
Bernadottes, 64.1a*
Bernhardt, S. 27.97, 180a; 31.348a, 367, 383, 399; 33.-351; 47.95a, 297, 580, 827; 61.636: 62.306
Bert, P. 33.272, 385, 405, 425, 427
Berthelot, 33.45
Besant, W. 63.475
Bible, [see N. T.] English, w 33.219a; criticism, 19.-408
Bibliografy, w 33.94
Bicycles, 63.281*
Biddle, G: W. 33.334¶
Bidwell, W. H. 97.720
Bigamy case 33.167
Bigelow, M. T. 33.102
Bikelàs, D. 32.225¶
Billee Taylor, 32.133
Billiards, 33.415, 426
Billings, dr. 33.238
Bimetalism, see Silver
Biografies, venal 33.196
Biology, 33.233
Bird, I. L. 27.211; 31.466; 62.635
Birds, 17.386a, 651a; 48.429; 63.25a*; 64.65a*; 97.643a; destruction, 150.506
Birdsall, E. q 33.253
Birney, J. G. w 33.254
Bismarck, 33.190, 291
Björnson, 31.275; q 32.44; *w* 28.318; 33.54, 294; 48.569
Black, W: 27.526; 31.346; 33.137; 48.572
Black Hills, w 33.340
Blackie, J. S. 31.430; 47.-858†
Black-mail, 33.387*⁎*
"*Blackwood,*" 32.113
Blaine, 32.19, 52, 67, 214, 289; 33.284**; 301, 406, 484
Blake, W: 47.289, 717
Blanc, mrs. 33.85
Blanchard, T. 63.254a*
Blanqui 17.273
Blauvelt, A ps 11.494
Bleichröder, 33.135*⁎*
Bliss, G: 31.419; 32.288; 33.-287; q 33.82, 284
Blood cir, discov. ps 11.294a
Blowitz, 63.845*
Blue Glass, ps 11.109
Blum, R. 48.196††
Boar hunting, 61.870a*
Bock, A.., 31.359, 377
Bodensee, w 33.56
Bodenstedt, q 33.135; *w* 32.-25§, 96§
Bodley, R. L. 32.716
Bodysnatching, 33.445
Boers, see Transvaal
Boisgobey, 32.302¶
Boits, 31.394
Bonaparte, J. (Patterson) 11.120a; N. 32.76; 97.396a; 150.629a; N. J. 33.85; S May, 33.227
Books, 33.448a; w 32.219; 47.-586; binding, w 31.469; buying (fancy prices) 33.-134; "illustrated," w 32.-406; love of, 97.407a
Book-trade, cheap libraries, 47.585
Bookwalter, q 33.82
Boole, G: 17.840a
Booth, E. 33.265; 63.61a*, 466
Borneo, w 33.96
Borrow, G: 150.817; 151.-114a, 560a
Borthwick, A. 64.43*
Boscobel 33.387
Boston, *Banks*, Pacific, 33.-406; woman's 31.249a, 280,

Figures to the left of the period indicate the vol. as follows: 10.11, Int. Rev.; 12-20, Pop. Sci.; 23, Century; 27.8, Lip.; 31.3, Nation; 47.8, Atl.; 62-4, Harper; 97, Eclectic; 149-51, Living Age.

806; 48.111a, 121a; 1st *church*, 33.9; mech. *fair*, 33.146, 304; *hist.* w 31.329, 417; 32.265 (records) 32.-206; *Society* 62.381a*
Boulger, D. C. 33.335
Boutwell, G: S. q 33.261
Boxford, Mass., 32.305
Boycott, 31.350
Boyd, C. E. 33.78
Boyesen, 32.303‡; 33.436
Bradlaugh. 32.327; 33.65, 107, 108a, 129, 187, 465
Bradley, G: G. 33.167, 347
Brady, 32.287, 290, 307, 325; 33.62
Brahmo Somaj, see India, *church*
Brahms, 32.13
Brain, overwork, ps 10.326a; 20.102a; 97.704a; reflex action, 1.544a; size, 16.829
Bramwell, sir G: 33.468a
Brandes, 32.114
Brandy, ps 10.428a
Brassey, T: q 33.387
Brauwer, 61.845a*
Brazil, hist. 33.427, 443; soc. 27.82a
Bread, 97.688a
Bread-stuffs, crops, 31.409; 33.65; export, 11.450a; 33.-185; "corner" 33.144
Brehm, 33.374
Bremen, 33.285
Brewster, A.. H. 27.619a; B. H. 33.482
Bridgman, F. B 32.95; 63.-694*; w 33.232
Brigandage, 33.176
Bright, J: 33.407
Brinley ly. 32.205, 259
Bristol, riot, 151.703; R. I. w 32.227
Broca, P. 20.261a*
Brockett, L. P. 33.240
Brockhaus lexikon, 33.316
Broglie, C. V. de 28.462a*
Bronsart, 32.27
Brook, S.. 33.456; farm, 61.-634; 62.147
Brooke, S. B. 47.441
Brooklyn, art, 31.445; repub. club, 32.343
Brougham, J: w 32.305
Brown, B. W. 31.382; J. E. 31.386; *P.* 32.229; W, 33.504
Browning, O. H. 33.128; R. 23.190*; *w* 23.189a; 33.415
Brownlow J: 150·190**
Brucke, E. 32.114
Brugsch, 32.313; *w* 31.314¶
Brunetiere, 47.418
Brush, G: J. 20.117a*
Buchanan, "dr," 32.215; J. 23.289a; 33.433
Buck, D. 62.811*
Buckley, B. 32.249
Buckner, col. 32.52
Buddism, w 32.261: 33.234; 48.840; lit. 33.117
Buchner, G: 32.224
Bürger, 47.161
Buffaloes, 17.40a
Bugge, 33.153
Buildings, safety, 61.305
Bulgaria, 32.381, 399; 33.3, 25, 43, 45, 63; 150.347
Bull, O. 61.308; 62.241*
Bunce, O. B. 97.712
Bunsen, R. W. 19.550*
Bunyan, 97.45**
Burano, 151.635a
Burbridge, 33.96
Burch, col. 33.81
Burial, 4.592a; law, 8.322a; places, 16.673a; 19.657a; premature, 16.67a; 317.527
Burke, 33.135
Burnand, F. C. 63.661*

Burnett, 47.861
Burney, miss 33.217
Burns, 47.518; 61.320*
Burroughs, 33.16
Burton, J: H. 151.161; *w* 33.-413
Busbecq, w 32.211a
Bushnell, H. 10.13a; 33.49; 47.126
Butler, B. F. 31.279; q 33.-301, S. A. 19.843
Butterfield, C. W. 33.421
Butterworth, H. 33.160
Buxton, R. H. 33.336
Byerly, W. E. 33.353
Byron, 47.521; w 31.344; *w* 62.145; ed. 33.122
Cable [see At. Tel.] *G. W.* 31.415; 33.54
Caddy, 33.357
Cailleux, T. q 33.276
Caird, J. q 33.407
Cairns, 32.367
Calamary, 149.768
Calculus, w 33.255
Calderwood, H. 63.471
Caldwell riot 33.443, 445, 485
Califate, 150.707a; 151.172a
California, survey, 32.27; trav. w 33.450; Tulu ilands 27.628; ranch, 27.366a; finance, 32.372; labor question, 17.433a; ry. monopoly, 33.22, 452a
Calvert, G: H. 31.450
Campanini, 62.807*; *w* 48.-281§§
Campbell, lord, w 32.222a; C. 33.65; *H.*. 32.339
Campbellites, 33.8, 49, 73
Campello, count, 33.263
Canada, *hist.* cont. 33.285, 427; w 31.340; *pop.* 33.107; French, 48.771a; *society,* court, 63.213a*; *sport,* 28.-399; 63.823a
Canals, N. Y. 32.160; 33.186
Canoes, 61.395a*
Canterbury, 48.813a
Caoutchouc mfg 17.802
Cape Colony diamonds, 27.-217a; hist. 31.435
Capponi, w 32.321
Cardiff giant, 13.197a
Caricature, w 32.390
Carleton, W. 33.14†
Carlisle, Pa., school, 62.-669a*
Carll, L. B. 33.255
Carlos, don, see Madrid
Carlyle, 32.94, 109a, 186**, 201a, 206, 243, 327**, 33.116; 47.721*,*, 863**; 62.883a*, 944**a; 97.289a; 150.85a**, 259a, 499; w 32.278; 33.38; *w* 27.413, 525; 32.291a; 33.-18, 199‖; influence, 62.-787; humorist, 48.463a; library 32.316
CARLYLE, 149.643
Carpenter, M. 32.142; W: B., 1.745a*; *W. H.*, 32.244
Carpenters, hist. 17.233a
Carpio, 47.63
Carr, gen. 33·186; *L* 32.259
Carrington, H: B. 33.332
Carrying trade, see Shipping
Carter, R. B. 151.451; *S. N.* 32.186
Carthage, w 33.160
Cary, A. L. 62.808*
Casey, A. 33.235
Catholic church [see Papacy] 149.650; hist. 31.334; 33.3; 151.387a; and schools, 8.495; 32.279
"Catholic World" 32.10
Catons, 61.489a*
Cattle, 61.93a; driving, 27..

Figures to the left of the period indicate the volume as follows: 1.9, 12-20, Popular Science; 10.11, International Review; 28, Century; 27-8, Lippincott's; 31.3, Nation; 47.8, Atlantic; 62-4, Harper; 97, Eclectic; 149-51, Living Age.

565a; 28.618; raising, 19.-835; w 32.190
Caucus, 33.261, 368a, 388a, 431, 463a, 483, 486a
Caux, G. de 33.326
Cecilia, St. 61.809a*
Cellier, A. 47.363
"Century" 23.143
Cervantes, 47.61; *w* 32.73¶
Cesnola 32.74, 95; 33.85
Chadwick, sir A. w 33.458
"Challenger" 31.394, 427
Challoner, R 47.431
Chalmers, dr. 150.499; H. H. q 32.132
Chamberlain, B H 32.98; J. L., 32.2
Chambrun, q 33.72
Chamisso, 32.167¶
Champlin, J D 31.462; 33.122
Chandler, C: F. 16.833a*
Chandler, P. W 33.77‖; W: E. 32,231, 359; 33.62
Channing 61.141
Chapin, dr 62.623
Character study 47.724
Charities, admin. 32.345a
Charleston, 28.49a; schools, 32.308
Charms, 64.97a*
Chasles, M. 18.840*
Chemistry, molecules, 97.-115a
Cheney, E D 33.9
Chess-playing 33.227
Chetwynd, H W 31.417§
Cherbuliez 32.301
Cherokees, 27.195a
Cherubino, 97.665
Chicago, 61.711a*; hist. 32.-252
Child, L. M. 31.309
Children, [see Babies] diseases, 17.249a
Chili, hist. 33.305, 327, 461, 464
Chillicothe, 63.853a*
Chimborazo, 32.133
China, w 31.293, 32.245a; *hist.* w 33.335a; 1862, 11.-518; cont., 33.445; Russia, 33.187; *edu*, sci. 149.633; *lit.*‡ 47.725; *soc.* 16.270a; 19.843; *tel.* 33.305
Chinese abroad, 27.404a; in U. S. 10.51; Brooklyn, 32.-8; Cal. 32.134a; servants, 27.261a; students, 33.45
Chinon 61.820a*
Chios, 32.253
Chloral, 15.491a
Chordal 32.79
"Christian Intelligencer," 32.74
Christian religion, 97.433a; 149.649a
Christie, E 31.255; W. H. M. 33.117
Christmas cards, 32.150
Chronicle of 1880 32.167
Chronology, 18.760a
Church F. J 31.375
Church in U. S. [see Mormons] anglican, 31.317; 33.64, 326, 346; w 32.65; [hist] 10.314a; congreg, w 47.277; Sci. edu., 6.735
Cibber 97.51**
Cicero w 33.75
Cinchona, 17.507a
Cincinnati, hist. 32.252; music 33.274; S. ry. 33.186
Cissey, 31.387
Cities [see Towns] 62.122a; govts, (Mass.) 33.169a, 196; refuse, 18.585a
Civil Service, *Eng.*, exams. 12.152a; *U. S.* (Eaton) 27.580a; 28.208; 31.316

Figures to the left of the period indicate the volume as follows: 1-9, 20-21, Popular Science; 10-11, International Review; 23, Century; 27-8, Lippincott's; 31-3, Nation; 47-8, Atlantic; 62-4, Harper; 97, Eclectic; 149-51, Living age.

836a, 392, 404a, 436a, 458; 32.5a; 10.54a, 258*,*, 328a, 362a, 371; w 32.316; 33.-472; before 1776, 32.258; *agitation*, 31.402, 408, 410, 420, 433, 451; 32.68, 122, 149, 162, 180a, 196, 204, 252, 270, 272, 307, 350; 33.-25, 26a, 42, 46a, 64, 65, 66a, 72, 84, 86a, 93, 163, 164, 224, 242, 261, 284, 343, 346, 248, 386, 404, 406, 441, 444, assessments, 32.400a; 33.323 369a; bills, 32.19; burden, 33.183; exams. 33.42, 61; pressure, 33.130a; tenure in N. Y. 33.154
C. S. pub. soc. 31.340, 357; reform asso. 31.371; 33.-126, 128
Civiletti, B 63.82a
Clapp, H C 64.151
Claremont, 61.224*
Claretie 32.319
Clarke, J: S 28.497a
Clay, C M 33.196
Clayton 47.546
Clémenceau, 31.351, 32.21
Clergymen, want of eloquence, 48.282; sci. edu., 6.735
Cleaveland, H. W. S. q 33.-432
Clifford, N. 33.62; 33.65; W. R., 15.258a*
Clyde, lord, w 32.353
Coal, 14.337a; ind., U. S. 33.-116; supply, 33.135
Coast-service, U. S. 15.182a*; 32.334, 406
Cobb, J. S. 32.463
Cobbe, F.. P. 32.174
Cobden club, 32.21; 33.285
Cockburn, A. 10.397a
CODMAN, J. 61.ii**
Coe, G: S. q 33.126
Coffee-house co., N. Y. 32.-407
Coinage, debasement. 12.-581
Coincidences, 15.628a
Colds, 18.801a
Coleridge, 47.520
Coles case. 33.62, 64; E. w 33.495a
Collins, W. q 61.469
Collyer, R. q 31.403
"Colonel," author, see Bruce
"Colonels," 32.244
Colonization, 11.88a
Color, 28.417; blindness, 19.-91a; 32.11; w 31.360; in sexes, 33.214
Colorado, archæ. 16.666a; trav. 47.46a; cattle, 28.618; floods, 33.128; indians, 32.-73; mining life, 10.518a; ranch cure, 28.90a
Colt, J. D. 33.128
Columbus, 151.643a
Combe, G: 15.109a
Combs, L. 33.147
Comets, 32.260; 33.75; 79.-256; 150.760a
Complexion and climate, 17.-1a
Coney iland, 33.84
Confederate bonds, 33.327, 346, 364, 366, 384, 427
Congdon, C. T. 32.47; 47.-565
Conger, O. D. 32.19
Congo expl. 33.198
Conkling, 11.375a; 31.280, 419; 32.19, 83, 104, 121, 142, 214, 232, 341, 359, 362a, 379, 382a, 397; 33.1, 22, 66a, 242, 244, 261, 281; q 31.246, 451; 33.82
Connecticut, 33.284; courts, 33.326; prison, 27.290a
Conscience, 13.513a; 14.647a; in beasts, 9.80a; H: 33.112

Figures to the left of the period indicate the volume as follows: 1-9, 12-20, Popular Science; 10-11, International Review; 23, Century; 27-8, Lippincott's; 31-3, Nation; 47-8, Atlantic; 62-4, Harper; 97, Eclectic; 149-51, Living Age.

N. Y. Nation - 1881 -

Consolations, 150.248a
Constant, B. 33.427
Constantinople, 33.427
Conversations-Lexikon, 33.-317
Conway, M. D. 33.299
Cook, C. 32.413; *D*, 33.516; J. 12.495a 18.556; 32.327, 350, *w* 63.471
Cooke, G. W. 33.396; J. P. ps. 10.746; *R. T.* 33.257
Cookery, 28.417; w 27.528; schools, 13.625: 97.124a; 149.689a
Cooley, T. M. 61.794
Coolidge, S. 31.431; 47.429
Cooper, E: 32.2
Co-operation, Eng. 17.742a; dress asso. 33.265
Cope, E: D. 19.110
Coppee, H: 02.282
Copper product, U. S. 33.-232
Copyriht, 13.618; 14.166a, 296a, 440a, 530; 19.372; 33.257 int. 10.746; 15.265; 16.697; 17.121, 554; 31.420, 442a, 459a; 32.33, 226a; 33.-229, 245, 366; 61.469; 62.-946 (dramatic) 33.224
Coquelin, 32.130¶, 407
Cordova, 28.344a*
Corea, hist. 33.427
Corfield, W. H. 32.198
Corinth canal, 33.35
Corneille, 47.64
Cornell univ. crew, 33.85, 129, 145, 147, 185, 186, 207, 208, 285
Corners, 33.210a; and law, 33.302, 307a; in Eng. 33.-227
Cornwall, trav. 63.801a*
Corwin, B. R. 31.453; 32.42; *O. von* 31. 425
Cossa, L. 32.212¶; P. 43.187
Costume col. 43.428
Cotton *crop,* U. S. 33.34, 284; *cult.* 11.350, 63.719a*; w 33.232; *ind.* Eng. (corner) 33.227, 263; French, 33.327
Courts, English, 33.468a; U. S., *criminal,* w 33.175; *federal,* supreme, 28.423a; 31.441a, 459; 32.8a, 26; 33.-441, 481, 504; dist. attorneys, 33.491; *bar,* 32.370; edu., 33.144
Cowley, E: 33.64
Cox, sir G: W. 33.491
Coxe, E. B. 32.20
Craddock, C: E. 32.372
Craik, D. M. 32.319†; 47.-858
Cramer case, 33.186, 208, 245, 265, 304, 326, 426
Crane, W. 33.15†
Crawfurd, O. 31.343; 63.470
Crédit mobilier, 33.387
Cremation, 150.640
Cricket, 33.265
Crime, 15.656a; 33.414; 150.-753; origin, 2.589a; 48.452a; and sex, 8.727a
Crimean war, 150.170*,*a; w 31.379
Criticism, 97.420*,*
Cromwell, w 33.474a
Crookes, W.. ps 10.739
Crops, [see Breadstufs] abroad, 33.45; Canada, 33.-265; U. S. 33.836
Crosby, H. q 33.105
Cruel, R. 31.464
Cuba, trav. 32.312a; fi. 33.-245; hist. 33.285, 305, 347, 367, 407

Figures to the left of the period indicate the volume as follows: 1-9, 12-20, Popular Science; 10-11, International Review; 23, Century; 27-8, Lippincott's; 31-3, Nation; 47-8 Atlantic; 62-4, Harper; 97, Eclectic; 149-51, Living Age.

Cucheval-Clarigny, q 33.-211a
Culture, 48.284; hist. 149.-643a
Cumberland, trav. 28.ii*
Cumming, G. 33.318
Curchod, S. 97.453a
Curteis, A. M. 32.156
Curzola, 151.59a
Custom-houses, U. S., useless 32.132; 33.423, 426
Cuyp, A. 61.61a*
Cyprus, 33.30, 425; archæ. w 32.259; in 1395, 150.126; lan, 32.95
Dakota 33.406
Dale, R. W. q 31.393
Dall, C. H. q 33.450; *w* 33.-400§
Dalmatia, trav, 150.824; *hist.* 151.59a; cont. 33.25
Daly, A 31.378§§
Damrosch 33.454
Dances, 27.330a*
Danford, 33.445
Dante, 47.59; *w* 31.397¶; *w* 149.651; soc, 32.112, 205
Dantzig meeting, 33.209, 325
Darc, J 63.91a
Darmesteter, J 33.438
Dartmouth college, 33.44, 84
Darwin, C: 32.17; 33.519; 64.149; 151.433
Daudet, A 33.305, 331, 379a
Davenport. F.. 47.363; J: 31.265; *J. I.* 32.355
Davids, T. W. R 32.261; 33.234
Davidson, T: q 32.403
Davin, N. F. 32.370; q 32.-332
Davis, D. 32.178, 213, 270; 33.302, 304; *J.* 33.10, 216; 48.405; J. C. B., 33.483; W: R 13.625
Davitt 32.85
Davy, sir H. 14.813a*
Dawes, 32.51, 103, 232, 287, 344; q 33.65, 84, 86, 130
Dawson, J: W. 8.231*
Deaf, edu 11.503a; 19.84a, 394a
Death, 3.270a¶; 8.617 apparent, 18.401a
Deception, see Lying
Deems, C. F 33.24
De Forest, J. B. 33.381; *J. W.* 32.376
Deffner, M 32.208
Degrees, bogus, 32.215
De Jarnette, 33.167
De Kay, C: 32.319; 47.856
Delane, J: 63.846*
Delibes, L 32.293a
Delmonico, L 33.186
Deming, P 47.281
Dem. party, 31.248a, 252a; 32.92: 33.408a
Dengremont, M. 32.95
Denmark, agric. 150.323 a hist. 33.25
Denslow, 47.442
Denton J. B. 32.357
Des Cars 32.339¶
Deutsche Rundschau, 32.-114
Deville, H. S. 33.25
Devonshire, 61.1a*
DeWitt, J: w 33.37
Diamonds, art. 17.259
Dicey, A. V. q 33.251a
Dickens, 36.467*,*; *w* 33.-418**a
Dike, S. W. q 33.133
Dillon, J: 32.85; 33.187
Diman, J. L. 32.94; mem. 33.50; *w* 33.57‡‡; 48.696
Dingley, gov. 33.226
Disease, 4.569a¶; 14.639a; 19.-721a; germs, 20.244a; 151.-323a; heredity, ps 11.332;

15.433a; and emotions, 8.60a;—mind, 15.71a; strengthening, 150.752
Divination by birds, 32.148
Divorce, 11.139a; France, 32.123; U. S., 33.22, 49, 91a, 114a, 134, 424; (N. Y.) 33.282
Dixie, F 32.284
Doddridge, P w 32.340
Dodge, T. A 33.18
Dogs, ps 10.202a; 27.347*; 28.473; 48.430; 151.507; in lit. 97.174a
Dolet, w 32.267
Domestic economy, 14.395; w 14.239; instruction in 150.510
Donaldson, T: w 33.50
Donne, J: 47.385
Dorsey, S. W. 31.442**; 32.-103, 122, 287, 307, 342; q 32.21
Dostoievsky, 48.423a; *w* 27.-630; 32.308
"Doterel," 33.187
Dotterels, 97.643a
Doudan 47.420
DOUGLAS, F: 23.125a**; q 33.44
Douw, G. 63.177*
Dove, H: W: 16.261a*
Dowden, E 27.419; 32.135
Doyle, dr. w 47.562; J. T. q 33.113, 452
Drake S: A 63.955
Draper, J: W., 4.361a*; *w* 7.230; 9.112
Draper, L. C. 33.435a
Dreams, 61.97a, 781a; 97.-249a; 150.95a
Dress and helth, 17.182a; 19.145a; women's, 28.311; 62.589a; economy 64.123a
Drew, C. 33.336
Drowning, 13.93a; 19.369a
Dryden, 33.417; 47.389; w 32.337
DU BOIS REYMOND, 13. iii; 14.409
Du Bois Reymond, 13.361a*
Du Chaillu, 33.445; 63.951
Duels, 33.306a; S. C. 32.143; Va., 33.245, 302, 304, 503, 4
Dufaure, 150.445
Duffy, C. G. 31.464
Dulcigno, 31.387
Dulles, J: W 33.378
Dumas A. 2d, 10.530a; 31.-398; 32.127; 48.383; J. B. A. 18.257a*
Dunkers, 23.214a
Dutcher, S. B. 33.41
Dwight H: O 32.338; J. S. 63.947
"Dwight's Journal," 33.-217
Dye, W: M 32.77‖
Dyer, T. F. T. 33.221
Earl, J: 32.101
Earth, 97.275; hist. w 16.-816a; early ideas of, ps 10.-542a*; age, 9.649a; int. 17.-289a; quakes, U. S. 32.279
Eastern, q 31.365a
East Granby prison, 27.290a
Eating, over, 97.131
Eaton, D. B. q 32.371
Ebers, 31.255, 393¶; 32.225¶; 33.98, 373¶; 47.589
Eckhardt, 33.16; 61.148
Edes, B. L. 33.166
Edgefield, S. C. 33.346
Edinburgh, duke, attentat, 28.310
Edis, R. W. 32.175
Edison, 13.487a*
Edmunds, 32.35; q 32.36; 33.163
Education, [Bain] ps 10.-418 etc., 14.111; 16.197a; w

Figures to the left of the period indicate the volume as follows: 1-9, 12-20, Popular Science; 10-11, International Review; 23, Century; 27-8, Lippincott's; 31-3, Nation; 47-8, Atlantic; 62-4, Harper; 97, Eclectic; 149-51, Living Age.

17.560; and govt. 17.585a; 18.664a; 19.635a, 703;—helth 6.57a 13.217a;—love-affairs, 33.352a;—manual labor, 18.26a; classical, 4.371, 13.531a; 14.819; 15.631a, 33.487a; competition, ps 11.105a; cram, 11.239a; discipline, 7.699a; incentives, 6.748; industrial, 12.571a; 18.202a; languages, 12.152a; lib. 4.1a; 31.309; pressure, 16.645a; Quincy system, 61.941; sci. 7.513, 746, 13.187a, 537; 14.674; 16.849; 18.159a, 638
Edward, T: ps 10.594a*
Edwards, H. S. 33.101, 139; *J* 62.251
Egypt, *army*, Americans in, 32.77; *forein relations*, U. S. influ. 33.195a;—consular juris. 33.152a; *hist*, cont., 33.30a, 207, 209, 227, 245, 263, 285, 291a, 305, 31.1a, 327, 347, 367, 387, 407, 411a, 490a
Egyptology, 32.313a; 151.123, 189; w 33.155a; 61.637; stone age, 32.28, 59, 74; mummies, 33.132a
Ehrenberg, C. G. 14.668a*
Eidlitz, L. 33.515a
Election sermons, 32.149
Electric girl, 6.588a¶
Electricity, 151.121a; exhib. 33.305 therapeutics, 151.319
Eliot, C: W. q 17.553; G: 23.57a*; 63.912a*; *w* 10.ii; 27.204; 31.456a; 32.202; 62.629; 149.791a
Elliot, H. W. q 33.471
Ellis, G: H. q 33.413
Elm 33.407
Elton, W: 47.371
Ely, R. T. q 33.67
Elze, K 32.353
Elzevir, D* 32.75
Embacher F 31.428
Embroidery, art. 62.693a*
Embryology, w 33.221
Emerson, 62.388a*; *w* 33.396a
Emmette, R 32.230
Emotions, 4.552a¶ in prim. man 6.331a; expr. 97.676a
Enander, J: A 33.154
Encyclopædia Brit. 32.333; 33.115
Engineering, 8.33a
England, *trav.* 58.ii;* 47.401a; 61.1a*; 62.1a;* baths, 63.484a*; lakes, 62.1a*; (S) 62.211a*, 650a*; 63.801a*; foot, 150.607a; *agriculture*, 31.335; 33.163, 209, 407; future, 31.405a; land 33.5a, 263a;—bill, 33.265; *army*, 33.25, 45, 445; *church*, 47.405; cath., 97.37a; *con.* 62.114a; w 32.100; *courts*, 33.468a; bar 47.407; chancery estates & U. S., 33.329a; *education*, denom, 10.1a; sci. 8.281; ps 10.23a; 13.558; *finance*, nat. welth, 151.760; *forein relations*, hist. 33.328; 1840, 61.202; refugees, 149.823; Turkey, 33.29a; U. S., 1781, 64.62; *history*, w 33.377; clans, 151.95a; 18th cent. 47.567; w 33.417; recent, 33.97; cont., 32.40a, 58, 233, 235a, 271. 274a, 329a, 366a; 33.165, 167, 187, 192a, 247, 407; *navy*, 149.753a; *politics*, Commons,

Figures to the left of the period indicate the volume as follows: 1-9, 12-20, Popular Science; 10-11, International Review; 23, Century; 27-8, Lippincott's; 31-3, Nation; 47-8, Atlantic; 62-4, Harper; 97, Eclectic; 149-51, Living Age.

27.453a; w 33.157a; obstruction, 32.72a, 85, 87, 123, 164a; procedure, 32.-53: 33.165; society, 33.-23; *press*, 63.ii*; *society*, 47.409, 444; 18th century 61.471; 150.188; —filistinism, 47.548a; flunkeys, 63.-628; snobbery, 61.631; women, 150.13a; *sport*, Americans, 33.25; *tariff*, 33.305; fair-trade, 33.109a, 129, 144, 165, 185, 225, 227, 249a, 263, 270, 367; free—, 32.323

English channel tunnel, 33.-285

English language in U. S., 48.849; dic. 97.236a; 150.-239a; dialects, w 32.12, 298; elements, 47.479; frases, w 32.263; *words*, Americanisms, 47.698a; index expur., 32.183; blizzard, 32.184, 208, 220, 260; had rather, 31.323; 33.394; jack, 47.584; then, 47.728

English literature, early, w 32.167; essayists, 97.610a; 151.69a *fiction*, Americans in, 47.140; *letters*, 151.131a; *poetry*, w 32.-209a; anglo-gallic, 47.720; Lancashire, 149.747; sonnets, w 32.262a; *study*, 8.-221a; 14.81a; 17.145a, 553; *style*, 12.341a

Engraving, wood, w 33.-394

Enseignment, revue de 32.-242

Ephesos, archæ 7.223a

Erie canal, 63.415

Ernst, C. W. 32.25

Esposito, see Randazzo

Etching, 27.313; 32.93; 33.-374

Etheredge, w 32.219

Ethics, sci [see morals] 17.-324a

Ethnology, 33.253*,*

Etiquet, w 32.283; 33.279a

Eucalyptus, 7.344a; 12.662a;* 19.94a

Euphrata, Pa 23.209a

Euripidês 47.57

Europe, traveling, 61.302; *armies*, 11.1a; *hist.* 1840, 61.197a*; *society*, 97.257a; 150.3a; med. 49.1a

Euthanasia, 3.90a

Evans, J 33.437

Evarts, q 31.245; 33.183

Evidence, 8.570a; 13.53a

Evolution, ps 10.60a, 86a, 236; 12.175a; 14.266a, 320a, 409a; 16.101a; w 6.745; 11.51a; 32.393a; and character, 47.371a;—hair, 15.-250a; —immortality, 7.-46a;—morality, 15.124;—revelation, 1.188a; 97.577a

Ewart, J. A. 32.299**

Ewing E. P 31.450

Examinations, public, 33.-184

Explosives, 33.346

Exhibitions, int. 32.21

Express cos. & rys. 33.62

Extradition, U. S., forein, 33.243, 266a, 283, 344; interstate, 31.350

Eyes, 12.74a; 149.703; 151.-451a; siht, 1.457a; 17.711; w 32.191a; in dark, 1.735a; and print, 19.54a¶

Faces, abnormal, 8.73a

Fair Trade, see England, *tarif*

Fairbairn, 19.846

Figures to the left of the period indicate the volume as follows: 1-9, 12-20, Popular Science; 10-11, International Review; 23, Century; 27-8, Lippincott's; 31-3, Nation; 47-8, Atlantic; 62-4, Harper; 97, Eclectic; 149-51, Living Age.

Falke, 33.394
Family, evolution, ps 11.-129a; future, ps 11.513a
Fargo, W. G. 33.106
Farragut statue, 32.389
Farrar, C: S. 33.479
Farrer, J. A. 32.377
Fashions, barbarous, 17.-711a
Faulmann, K 32.221
Fausset, A. R 31.277
Faust, w 32.242
Fawcett, E 31.353§§; 32.-169§§; 47.364§§; 48.561; 97.713; H. 31.247
Fay, A 32.395
Feathers, 15.367a
Federlein, G 32.66
Felix, R. w 47.835
Fels zum Meer 33.331
Fenton, J: 33.203
Feuardent, 32.74, 90, 334
Feurbach, 33.294
Feuillet, 11.428a; 33.54
Fever, 14.143a; tree [see Eucalyptus]
Fiction, 47.585; 97.78a; in libraries, 33.33, 153, 370a, 512; plots, 63.146; writing, 48.570
Fiction 33.197
Field, C. W. 33.262; q 33.41; D. D., 33.144; K., 33.265
Fields, J. T. 32.298; 33.514a; 48.253a; 62.391*; 63.305
Fiji, w 33.318a
Fillmore, M. 47.538a; wife, 33.128
Filology [see Language] comp. 47.478a
Filosofy, anc. w 33.338
Filtration, 16.495a
Finance [see America, etc. *Finance*] public dets, 10.-210a
Fink, A., q 32.160
Fire [see Heating] places, w 32.149
Fires in U. S. 33.208; causes, 14.653a
Fiske, J: q 32.10, 60; *w* 6.-367; 47.583
Fishing, 28.268a, 529a*; 47.-844a; w 33.18, 160
Fitch, A 16.116a*; *J. G* 32.-340
Fleming, G: 27.215; 32.16: 47.587, 707
Flint, A 9.103*
Flipper, 33.164, 166, 184, 186, 248a, 269, 366, 385, 464
Florence, hist. 150.643a; w 32.66; schools, 151.341a
Floriculture, 22.219a*
Florida, hist. 31.297; land co., 33.485; life, 27.508a
Flowers, 151.436; use, 47.-579; wild, 2.356a
Flying machines 8.453a
Foley, J: 33.24
Folger, 33.343
Folk lore, 27.523; w 32.261a, 280; diffusion, 48.310a; negro, 18.824a; 7 sleepers, 61.547a*; water, 150.809 etc
Fontes Comparationis 32.-299
Food, 1.309a¶; 3.441a; 14.-721a; 15.30*,*a, 347, 377a; 28.231a; 97.688a; adulteration (legislation,) 32.52; condiments, 1.701a¶; Greek, 150.498a; school-children's, 1.590a; use, 14.-799a
Forbes, A 63.669; *A* 32.268; J. M. q 31.300, 316
Forney, J: W. 31.279; q 32.-85; *w* 32.155**

Figures to the left of the period indicate the volume as follows: 1-9, 12-20, Popular Science; 10.11, International Review; 23, Century; 27-8, Lippincott's; 31-3, Nation; 47-8 Atlantic; 62-4, Harper; 97, Eclectic; 149-51, Living Age.

Forestry, 19.830a; 33.432; w 32.339; U. S., 33.426; 48.-682a; w 32.339; schools, 19.311a; 33.370a.
Forests, 19.176a; fires, 32.-364; hyg. value, ps 11.385a; and rain, 7.207
Forrest, E. w 33.298
Forrester, A 43.226
Fortune bay, 31.421; 32.-399
Fortuny, 23.15a*
Fosforesence, 16.804a
Foster, gov, 33.65; J: W. 33.366; S. G. 62.66*; S. S., 33.216; *W* 33.472
Fothergill, J. 31.316; *J. M.* 33.294
Fowler, T: 31.396; W: H: 33.321
Fox, C: J. 10.274a; 62.419a; w 31.412a; 47.567; hunting, U. S., 31.287a; 33.28
Foxton, E. 47.428
"Français, le," 31.253
France, *travels*, (C) 61.381, 820a*; (N E) 28.539a*; *army*, 33.271; *bank*, 33.-407; *church*, 33.427, 62.-573a; and govt, 31.387, 406a; 33.271; *constitution*, 10.463a; 62.573a; reform, 33.107; *courts*, 31.371 *education*, bill, 33.25; schools, 97.413a; women, 31.439; *finance*, 33.211a, 429a; assignats, 9.615a; *forein relations* 31.287; Italy, 33.65; *history*, w 33.198a, 497; 1848, 151.53; cont., 31.247, 251, 281. 320a, 351, 387; 32.6a, 21; 33.265, 305, 307a, 366, 385, 387, 407, 409a, 427, 483; 150.347; *politics*, 61.790; legitimists, 33.65; scrutin de liste, 32.197, 346a, 361; women, 31.439a; *press*, 27.177; 31.373; law, 33.45; *society*, 33.255; domestic, 48.164a; riding, 33.434; women 150.7; 151.671a; *stage*, 27.383a; w 33.376; amateur, w 33.94; monolog, 23.312; tragedy, 47.-289a; *tarif*, 33.145; and Eng. 32.331; 33.189a, 225, 227, 265, 367, 407
French *language*, names, 62.430a; *lit*, chansons de geste, 32.28; obscene, 31.-355a; sentimentality, 47.-729
Francillon, 32.302
Frankland, E: 15.838
Franklin, B. w 33.373; Mss. 32.60, 389, as scientist, 31.-463; 61.265a;—J: w 33.-300
Fraser, A C 33.19
Fraunhofer, J 6.739*
Frazer, H. L. q 32.219
Freeman, E: A: q 33.493; *w* 31.295, 342; 33.256, 454; 47.83
Free Trade [see England, etc., tarif] 33.205; Australia, 33.243
Frelinghuysen, 33.461
Fremont, 33.304
French H. W. 32.172; 47.-713
Frenology, 14.475a; 18.599a¶; w 32.174
Frere, B 31.435
"Fresh," 32.146a
Freytag 47.575
Friederici, C. 32.353
Friedrich Wilhelm III, wife, 61.197*; IV, 61.199*
Frost, H. F. 33.139

Froude, q 31.247; *w* 10.116a; 97.159a
Fruit and forests, 2.194a; Cal. 33.471
Fuel, see Heating
Furness, H. H. 31.327
Furniture, easy chairs, 14.186a
Furs, 4.143a*
Fyffe, A. C. 32.76
Fysiology, instruction, ps 11.669a
G*aboriau,* 33.99
Gaelic lan. 33.192
Gagneur, 33.99¶; 48.568
Galiani, 33.230**
Galileo, ps 10.385a¶
Gambetta, 31.351; 33.29a, 147, 165, 167, 187, 193a, 251, 307a, 347; 97.345a; 150.345; q 33.107
Games, 28.629; 31.131a; 33.173; hist., 15.225a
Gamgee, A 31.432
Ganette, 33.436
Gannet, H: q, 33·415
Gardens, 62.515a*; w 33.420
Gardiner, S: R' 33.377
Garfield, 23.168a*; 28.520; 33.4a, 228a, 241, 214a, 293, 357a; 48.707; 63.949; 97.544; 150.571a; w 31.257; 33.294†; q 31.402; *w* 23.316; 33.326, 331, 426, 455; abroad, 33.71a, 223, 241, 244, 264, 285, 289, 291, 305, 327, 347, 407; eagle, 32.69; dog, 32.161; wife, 32.167; murder, 33.1, 24, 41, 44, 48, 64, 81, 84, 103, 106, 125, 128, 143, 146, 163, 166, 183, 186, 208, 210a, 223, 226, 241, 244; 48.395a; 63.624; (abroad) 33.71a, 223, 241, 244, 264; treatment, 33.244, 264, 284, 493; funeral, 33.386; monument, 33.346, 406; fund, 33.26a, 41, 244, 284, 326
Garrison, w 47.558
Gartenlaube 33.276
Gas, ps 10.478a
Gascoigne, 33.360
Gasparin, w 33.159¶
Gay, S. H., 10.494‖; 32.247
Geddie, J 33.458
Gegenwart, 32.221
Gem books, 32.390
Genealogy, 13.583a
Genesis, 33.253
Geneva award, 10 436a
Genève, hist. 151.380
Genius, 150.752; heredity, 32.131; 47.371a
Geografy, w 33.295; exhib. 33.187; history, 16.236a; study, 3.389; continents, 97.58; Royal Society, 33.374
George III, family, 61.511a*; IV, w 33.52a; 63.145; *H.* 16.721a
Georgia, hist. 31.280
Geraldine, 33.473
Germania theater, 33.227
Germany, [see Rheinland, Thüringen] *travels,* 28.228a*; 61.38a*; 150.703; *agriculture,* 16.467a; 150.373; *army,* 11.1a; *church,* med., w 31.464; cath. 31.286a; 33.250a, 508a; and govt. 33.187, 189a, 194a, 245, 290; *constitution,* 63.591a; *finance,* 31.374a; credit unions, 47.207a; mortgages, w, 31.277; *history,* cont, 32.179,

Figures to the left of the period indicate the volume as follows: 1-9, 12-20, Popular Science; 10-11, International Review; 23, Century; 27-8, Lippincott's; 31-3, Nation; 47-8 Atlantic; 62-4, Harper; 97, Eclectic; 149-51, Living Age.

383; 33.7a, 105, 129, 187, 227, 346, 349a, 365, 392, 405, 407, 409, 425, 443, 445, 470a, 485; 150.348; *library*, nat., 33.51; *politics*, Jews, 31.-371, 403, 438a; 33.165; *population*, pesants, 48.-307; *press* and U. S., 31.375, 459; 32.25; belles-lettres, 33.275, 434; *railways*, 33.-67; society, 150.489a; hist. 150.16; character cf with French, 33.255; cook school, 97.124a; 149.689a; marriage, 48.286; (law) 47.36*‚*‡a; out door life, 27.43a; village, 16.467a; women, 48.141; *tarif*, 31.-409; 33.265; timber, 31.292

German language, w 31.342; spelling, 32.29

Gerster, E., 62.806*; *w* 31.-291, 326

Gibbon, 97.57. 453a; 150.-579a; *w* 97.57**

Gibbons, W. G., q, 32.130

Gibraltar 33.427

Gibson, *W* 32.319; *W. H.*, 31.427

Gift, T. 28.112; 33.54

Gilbert, W. S. 33.298; 47.-363

Gilder, J. B. 31.357; *R. W.*, 31.431

Gill, D 33.94; *W:* 31.293

Gipsies, 16.540a; w 33.358

Girton college, 97.134

Glaciers, 151.447

Gladden, W 23.318‡‡

Gladstone, 33.345, 347; q, 33.283, 285

Glass, 7.554a; mfg, U. S., 32.334; blue [*q. v.*] 33.272

God and nature, 17.27a

Godefroy museum, 8.699a

GODKIN, 48.395

Goeler von Ravensburg, 32.14

Goethe, 47.161; w 32.285, 408; 33.101; *w* 33.181**; 149.657; 151.246**a; music, 32.200a; science, 17.-215a

Goff, N. 32.20

Gold coin 33.267

Goldoni, 151.259a

Goldschmidt, J 31.277

Goodale, 31.431; 33.32

Goody 2 shoes, 33.374

Gordon, col., w 33.97, 213; *J. E. H.* 32.33

Gorridge q 32.330a

Got, 33.107

Gottschalk, 28.630¶

Gould, J. 31.434; 32.84; 33.-424; q 32.142

Gounod, 62.468

Gowen 32.1

Grace, W. R. 31.281

Grady, H: W. q 33.232

Graham, T., see Lynedoch

Grant, D. q 33.387; O. L. 33.106; U. S., 31.297; 32.-51, 103, 215; q 31.245; 33.-22; fund, 31.369; 32.196

Gray, E., 14.523a*; H. 33.-482; mrs. R. 47.543

Grayling, 28.268a

Greece, ANCIENT, survey, 33.233; *archæ*, 32.278; w 31.499; and govt, 31.289a; *society*, w, 32.137; culture, 149.644; dinners, 150.493a; MODERN, *brigandage*, 33.303; *edu.*, 31.-255; *history*, 1823, 151.-493; cont., 33.313a, 367; and Turkey, 31..453; 32.3, 53, 105, 161, 215, 271, 274, 289

Figures to the left of the period indicate the volume as follows: 1-9, 12-20, Popular Science; 10.11, International Review; 23, Century; 27-8, Lippincott's; 31.3, Nation; 47-8, Atlantic; 62-4, Harper; 97, Eclectic; 149-51, Living Age.

Greek *language*, study, 18.-412; modern, 32.208: *lit.* 149.646; w 47.288; monasteries Mss., 31.411; play [see Sophoklês]; poetry, modern. 151.482a
Green J. M. 33.208; *S. A.* 33.174
Greenbackers, 33.164, 166
Greene, F. V. 31.383
Greenland, 8.431a
Green mts. 62.641a*
Greenwich meridian, 32.-317; obser. reports, 32.12
Greenwood, F. 64.44*;—lake school, 33.24
Greey, E: 33.456
Gregorovius, q, 47.722
Griffis, 31.363
Grote, A: R. q 33.254
Groton, Conn. 33.208; Mass., w, 31.376
Grove, G: q 33.295; W. R. 7.363
Günther, C. L. G; *w* 33.220
Guerrier 31.313
Guiraud, P. q 33.494
Guiteau, 32.463, 464; 33.24, 48, 146, 166, 208, 223, 226, 244, 253, 264, 272, 281, 284, 301, 304, 326, 328a, 344, 346, 384, 386, 406, 408a, 423, 432a, 441, 444, 446a, 484, 502, 504
Guizot, w 48.413
Gunn, F: W 33.147
Gunpowder, 6.729a
Gymnastics, 13.129a; 19.7a
H*abberton*, 31.330
Haeckel, E. H: 31.108*
HAECKEL, 11.641a
Haldeman, S. S. w 33.115; *w* 33.334; ly. 32.259
Hale, E: E. 62.394; *w* 33.454, 478‖; N. 61.53a*
Halevy, L.
Hall, F. E: 32.94; 33.394; *G. S.* 32.184
Halliwell, 32.151
Halsted, G. B. 33.321
Hamburg, hist. 33.427
Hamilton, A. 31.445; G., 31.317; *w* 32.323‖; *W:* 33.-19
Hamley. E. B. 28.527‡
Hammond, J. H. 11.352; *W. A.* 63.631
Hampden, J: 33.231
Hampton school, 32.185; 61.-627a; 62.659a*; W. 31.280**
Hancock, W. S., 31.245, 263; 33.224
Hanging, 13.349a
Hannibal & St. Jo. ry., 33-205
Hanson, W: L 33.187
Harcourt, sir W: V. 63.844*
Hardcastle, 33.314
Hardy, A. S 33.393; *lady D* 33.519; *T*: 27.213; 32.16; 47.712
Harlow, R. P., q 32.295
Harmony, 16.508a
Haroun Alraschid, w 32.412
Harpers vs Scribners 32.205; mag., 31.325; 61.303; *62.-303; 63.789; (index) 32.130
Harris, J. C. 31.398; S. T. q 17.695
Harrison, G. J. q 33.105; *J. A.* 33.498‖
Hartig, q 32.3
Hartmann, E: von, 2.-152a¶; L. 33.83, 84, 104, 106, 146, 184, 187
Hartt, C. F. 13.231
Hartwig, 32.65
Harvard, univ., 32.75, 112; annex, 31.377; 62.101a; divinity school, 48.377a;

Figures to the left of the period indicate the volume as follows: 1-9, 12-20, Popular Science; 10-11, International Review; 23, Century; 27-8, Lippincott's; 31-3, Nation; 47-8, Atlantic; 62-4, Harper; 97, Eclectic; 149-51, Living Age.

Greek play, (see Sophoklês) print, 33.253; religion, 32.259; [agnosticism] 19.-267; study, 3.769; 17.482a; Yale race, 33.6a
Harvard Register, 32.242
Harvey, 13.396
Hase, R. 31.347¶
Hatherly, ld 33.25
Hatton, J. 33.202§
Hauff, 33.477
Hauk, M. 33.317
Havana, 32.312a
Hawaiian ilands, w 32.193; trav. 28.361a; hist. 33.43, 206; natives, 33.243
Hawker, R. w 48.571
Hawthorne, 63.260; w 61.-945
Hay, M. C. 32.411
Hayes, I. H., 33.453; I. I., 33.485; R. B. 31.315, 401; 32.68; mrs. 32.167; admin. 31.282; 32.144
Haynes, H. W. q 32.59
Hazen, W. B. 31.402
Hazlitt, 97.623; 151.79
Heard, F. F. 33.439
Heartlessness, 150.753
Heat, 33.45*⁎*; and helth, 3.-497a; *solar*, engines, 9.-550a
Heath, C: 32.287; *R:* 33.-176
Heating, 2.472a; 3.193a
Hedges claim, 33.329
Heilprin, 61.636
Heine, 47.163, 97.641; w 32.-64; mem. 32.76; *w* 33.159¶
Heinzen, K: 32.13
Hell, 12.627a
Hellenic Studies, 32.137
Helmholtz, 32.411¶; 151.-451¶
Helper, H. R. 33.47
Henderson, F. C. 33.99
Henry VIII., 10.116a; J. 2.-741*; 13.365; 32.406; P. 33.-49, 91
Henschel, G: 31.342; *T.* 31.-394
Henshall, J. A. 33.160
Henslow, J: S. 3.159*a
Hepworth, G: H. 33.99‡
Herbert of Cherbury, 97.50**
Herbst, W. 32.168
Herculaneum, 2.232a
Herculesbad, 33.270a
Herder, 31.415
Heredity, [see Evolution] 4.55a¶; 14.356a; 19.663; 32.131, 463; 47.377a
Hero-worship, 47.75a
Herring, 19.433a
Herschel, C. 8.736a*
Hershon, P. I. 32.156
Hervey, A. B. 33.159; 64.-153
Herzen, 33.119
Hewett, A. S. 31.391a
H. H. 32.152‖
Higginson, T: W. q 31.281, 317; 32.51, 71; 33.314
Hilgard, J. E. 7.617*; 33.501
Hill, F. H. 63.668; R., w 32.-138
HILLEBRAND, 97.257; 150.3; *w* 18.272; 31.414a; 47.421
Hiller, F., q 31.291
Hillern, 31.382
Hippopotamos, 149.637
Hirth, G. 32.333
History, primitive (see Palæontology) 16.545; 17.-495a; collec. documents, 33.511; pop. 31.450
Hiscock, 33.429
Hitchcock, sen. 33.25
Hoar, D. B. q 32.371; G: R., q 32.251

Figures to the left of the period indicate the volume as follows: 1-9, 12-20, Popular Science; 10-11, International Review; 23, Century; 27-8, Lippincott's; 31-3, Nation; 47-8, Atlantic; 62-4, Harper; 97, Eclectic; 149-51, Living Age.

Hobrecht, 33.305
Hocking valley coal, 33.124
Hodge, C. w 31.281; 47.560; 62.310
Hodgkin, T: 32.29
Holden, E: S. 32.118; 63.-312‖
Holladay, B. 32.35
Holland, *trav.* 32.170a; *crown*, heir, 31.428; *hist.*, 33.407
Holland, J. G. 23.161a*, 311a; 33.305, 315; 63.509*; 64.-147
Holmes, O. W. 31.312; 2d 32.286
Holst, 32.280a
Holyoake, G. J., 33.182
Home study Soc., y. m., 31.-444
Homer, birthplace. 33.276; W* 32.80
Hommel, F. 33.355
Hood, J. 33.34*
Hooft, 32.259
Hooker, J. D. 4.237*
Hooper, C. L. 32.304
Hope, A. R. 32.194
Hopkins, M. 63.545*
Horace, 32.79¶
Horn, F. W. 32.32
Horses, feet, 18.468; races, 32.398; 33.285, 304, 327; [Eng.] 28.72a, 33.227, 265, 410a; riding, 23.146
Horstmann, 33.117
House, E: H. 33.360
Household, [see Domestic Economy] art, w 32.413; 33.357
Housekeeping, co-op., 9.-733a; 48.331a
Houses, [see Heating, Ventilation] 4.69a; w 32.268
Houssaye, A. 32.220
Howard, B. W. w 33.436; C: H. 31.453; *O. O.* 33.95‖
Howe, J. W. 62.298*; T. O., 31.304; 33.482
Howells, W: D., 62.281*; w 32.11§§¶; 33.54, 154, 254, 333; 48.402; 63.637
Howgate, 33.143, 147, 166, 186, 326
Hubard, 32.16
Hubbard, J. M. q 33.370, 361
Huber, F., 6.486a*; V. A. 32.445a
Hubert, st. 61.692a*
Hudson, H. N. 32.338
Hueffer, F, 6.486a*
Huger, F. K., w 33.492
Hughes, T: q, 31.247; w 33.-59, 288
Hugo, w 33.249; w [Laugel] 11.ii; 31.407a, 457a; 32.7a
Huguenots, w 31.366
Hume, 149.655
Humming birds, 63.25a
Hungary, travels, 33.230, 270a; hist. 33.43; Germans, 31.446
Hunt, *A. W.* 27.527; 32.302; *L.*, 97.550†; T. S. 8.486*; q 31.1; 33.134; W: q 33.-493; W. M., 61.161a*
Huntington, G: P., q, 33.413
Hurlbut, 33.325, 364, 405, 461
Huxley, T: H: 4.739a*; q 31.309; w 11.527a; 33.175
Hydrofobia, 6.174
Hygiene [see Disease, Food] 2.665a; ps 10.198a; and cold ps 10.654a¶; 97.511; fallacies, 20.156a; instruction, 4.421; precautions, 20.56a; —soil, 33.295
Hypnotism, 3.618a¶; 9.211a; 18.108a

Figures to the left of the period indicate the volume as follows: 1-9, 20-21, Popular Science; 10-11, International Review; 23, Century; 27-8, Lippincott's; 31-3, Nation; 47-8, Atlantic; 62-4, Harper; 97, Eclectic; 149-51, Living age.

Iceland, con., 31.342; lit. w 32.244
Ichthyology, w 33.120a
Idols, 8.158
Ihne, 32.151
Ilands, water supply, 6.440
Iliohan, mrs. q 33.282
Illinois, hist. early, w 33.-495a; univ. 10.512a
Imagery, 18.64a
Imagination, ps 11 455a
Imitation, 15.656a
Imola, B. da., *w* 33.354
Inama Sternegg, *w* 32.45
Income tax, U. S. 32.84
Indexes, Q. P. 47.295; Annual, 33.373
India, *travels*, 2.614a; *church*, theistic, 31.464; 32.150; 151.423a; *history*, 1857, w 32.299; cont., 33.-187, 265; w 32.31; *society*, native, 150.227a; mental seclusion, 151.438; *sport*, 61.870
Indiana, hist., 31.279, 289a, 298
Indians, 27.195a; 32.67; 33.-406; w 33.320; cranium, w 32.259; education, 32.464; 62.659a*: and govt., 10.-380a; 31.401; 32.83, w 152a; 47.572; hist. cont., 33.65, 128, 147, 167: (war) 33.186, 208, 245, 265, 346; w 33.-95; lan. w 31.358
Indian Ter., 31.421; 32.380
Indigestion, 1.75a; and mind, 18.226
Infernal machines, 33.85, 87a, 104, 143
Ingelow. J. 27.424; 32.173, 183
Ingersoll, E. *w* 32.119; R., 31.315; 32.74
Insanity, 12.432a; in law, 1.-440a; 11.440a; 33.328, 446, 490; 48.780a
Insects, fossel, w 32.150
Institutions, early, 19.197a; 32.94; w 33.203; parliaments, 19.342a, 577a; English, 33.375; w 33.373; Germanic, w 32.45; 33.-135, 238‡‡a
Insurance, life, 19.732a; 62.-273a, 754a; hist., 19.482a; U. S. 33.51; graveyard, 33.-265, 387
Interior dept, 32.269, 307, 326; 33.501
Inventions, 16.755a
Iowa, hist., 33.44, 304
Ireland, [see Kelts,] *travels* [N] 27.321a*; [W] 62.-506a*; *question*, 10.ii; 11.-185a; 27.203; 31.247, 265, 319a; 62.148; w 33.135a; *history*, Eng., illtreatment, 32.204; 16th cent., 151.603a; recent. w 31.464a; cont., 32.52, 105, 123, 127a, 143, 161, 179, 309, 399; 33.23, 63, 65, 107, 128, 145, 164, 187, 206, 209, 225, 227, 243, 265, 267a, 283, 285, 293, 303, 305, 309a, 325, 345, 347, 367, 369, 371a, 405, 407, 425, 427, 445, 448a, 465, 485, 505; w 32.-188a; *industry*, 151.187; *land* q 32.21, 39a, 69; w 32.132; U. S. aid, 33.65; bill, 32.253, 355a, 288, 292a, 361, 381; 33.3, 23, 25, 43, 65, 83, 84, 89a, 105, 106, 167, 171a, 193, 249, 265, 347, 365, 387; "boycotted," 97.-209a; 150.113a; league, 33.-147, 302, 327, 329a, 365,

Figures to the left of the period indicate the volume as follows: 1-9, 12-20, Popular Science; 10-11, International Review; 23, Century; 27-8, Lippincott's; 31-3, Nation; 47-8 Atlantic; 62-4, Harper; 97, Eclectic; 149-51, Living Age.

445; *language*, 33.192; *lit.* †w, 33.477
"Iroquois," 32.398
Iron, 1.340a; founding, 62.-64*; industry, U. S., 32.-260; 33.233
Irving, 63.144
Irwin, H. C. 32.31
Isherwood, B. F. 32.317
Isle royale mines, 19.601a
Italy, travels, (C) 151.361a; map. 33.233; *church*, meth. 33.324; *education*, 151.341a; *finance*, paper. 31.440a; *foreign relations*, 33.3, 248a, 327, 347, 367; *history*, cont., 33.407; 97.-328a, 150.387a; *industry*, 32.369a; *politics*, suffrage, 33.111a; *press*, trial, 33.-509a; *society*, 150.256; Renas., 150.3a; 15th cent., 48.672a; holidays, 150.359a; rural, 151.736a; woman's edu., 47.722
Italian *language*, w 32.261; 33.474; Abruzzi dialect, 33.-35; *lit.*, early ‡, 33.10
Ithaka, archæ., 32.278
Jackson, C. 31.450; C: T. 19. 404a*; H. E. 32.68; *J.* 33.294
Jacobi, M.. P. q 32.387
James, E. J. q 33.353; *H:* 27.214; 31.358; 33.332; 47.-709, 871; 61.474; 63.627; T: L., 32.178, 342; *W:* 31.444; 32.131; judge, q 33.302
Janauschek, 32.208
Janney, L. N. 31.382
Janson, C. 33.355; *K* 47.286
Japan, w, 32.281a; 33.317; travels, 31.466a, 649a*; *archæ.* 14.257a*; 16.593a*; *history*, 10.477a; 33.347, 387; *industry*, silk, 33.-465; *population*, English, 33.73a; 47.610a; *literature*, †¶, 47.731; learned soc's., 151.632a; *society*, food, 33.514
Jaubert, 27.498a; 32.89; 97.-637a;
"Jeannette," 33.485, 505
Jefferson, J. w 33.516
Jeffrey, R. V. 32.98
Jennings, G: H: 33.157, 498; *L.* 150.611§
Jerez, M. 33.128
Jessup, A. D. 33.25
Jevons, W. S., ps 11.745; *w* 32.227
Jewell, M. 31.297
Jewels, 28.105; French crown, 33.465
Jewett, S. O. 33.479
Jews, 32.148; 33.325, 494; religion, 9.589a; hist. early w 33.208;—U. S., 32.327; Germany, 33.147, 213, 227, 347, 367; Russia, 32.327, 347; Servia, 33.445; Spain, 150.447; Syria, 33.187
Johnson, *E* 32.229; *H: P:* 33.295; *O.*, 33.413; S: w 32.12; *V. F.* 33.235
Johnstone, mr. 64.40*
Jones, T: 61.798; *W. B.*, 32.188
Jonquière *w*, 33.240
Joseffy, 62.812*
Journalism, 31.403; 62.144a; anon, 61.142; interviews, 61.306; 63.785
Judd, L. F. 32.193
Jullien, A. 32.79
Jumpers of Maine, 18.178a
Junius, 64.145
Jurisprudence, (see Institutions) comp. 17.577a

Figures to the left of the period indicate the volume as follows: 1-9, 12-20, Popular Science; 10-11, International Review; 23, Century; 27-8, Lippincott's; 31-3, Nation; 47-8, Atlantic; 62-4, Harper; 97, Eclectic; 149-51, Living Age.

Kaden, *W* 32.351; Kairwan, 33.366
Kalakaua, 33.206, 245
Kalas, 33.317
Kalloch, I. M. 32.214
Kangaroos, 8.409a*
Kansas, hist., 32.327, 443
Kant, 33.309a; cel., 33.24; *w* 11.357a
Kapp, F: q 31.342, 409
Kasson, q 33.384
Katcher, L. 32.32§.
Kayser, prof., 33.410a
Keeley motor, 33.485
Keifer, 33.444
Kelley, W. D. 33.501
Kelly, J: 31.336, 419, 422a
Keltic languages, 33.191a, 216
Kelts, pol. incapacity, 11.-185a
Kentucky farms, 63.124; hist. 32.52, 33.106
Kerfoot, bp., 33.25
Keyes, E. W. 32.2
Kiddle, H: 15.408
Kielland, A. L. 32.225
Kiepert, 33.284
Kilpatrick, 33.405, 465
King, *E*: 31.311†; *J. W.* 31.-293; S. A., 33.227
Kinglake, 31.379
Kipp, L. 31.172; 47.714‡
Kirkman, q 33.415
Kirkwood, 32.269
Klaczko, J. 32.155
Kleinpaul, 32.333
Kletke, H. 32.377†
Kluckholn, 33.393¶
Knox, R. 7.542a; *T. W.* 32.396, 405
Koerner, G. q 32.276
Korum, F. 33.194
Kossuth, 47.541
Kotzebue, 97.388a; 150.438a
Krapotkin, 33.167
Kraff, J. L. 33.505
Kwong, 32.263
Labiche,*** 47.729
Labor question, ps 11.-605a; 16.723a; w ps. 10.-109; asso's., 8.586a
Labouchere, 63.849*
Lace, 8.521a*
Lacour, 31.428
Lafayette fam., 150.749a
Lafontaine, 47.155
Lakes, 9.539a; *great*, canal communication, 63.415a*; fishing, 33.217
Lalanne, M. 32.266
Lamar, 33.206
Lamartine, 61.201*; w 33.-355
Lamb, C: 32.187; *w* 97.621; 151.77; *M. J.* 32.117
Lampros, S. 31.411
Landor, 47.521; w 28.422; 33.179a; 63.790
Landstad, M. B. 31.395
Lanfrey, 97.641
Lang, A. 33.39, 134
Lange, 33.294
Langlet, A. 33.94
Language (see Filology) 14.-191a; common, 33.176; origin, 48.655a; w 33.332; (imitative) 32.88; original 32.261; *study*, 6.322a¶; 7.-142a
Lanier, J. F. D., 31.370, 385, 408; 33.167; S., 33.-208, 216, 394; *w* 31.310; 61.-796
Lankester, E. R. 31.446, 467; 32.414
Lanza, 31.382
Lapham, E. G., 33.61; q 33.-64
Lappenberg, J. M. 32.285¶

Figures to the left of the period indicate the volume as follows: 1-9, 12-20, Popular Science; 10-11, International Review; 23, Century; 27-8, Lippincott's; 31-3, Nation; 47-8, Atlantic; 62-4, Harper; 97, Eclectic; 149-51, Living Age.

Larcom, 47.429
Larkin, H. q 33.116
Larned, 33.449
La Roche, K: 31.463
Lasaulz, A von, w 27.422; 32.412
Latin language, pronun, 11.-66a; *lit.*, †, w 33.842a; 48.-701
Laughter, 57.256
Law [see Crime, Institutions] *administration*, juries, 32.45; [civil suits] 48.9a; *profession*, [see Courts] cases on speculation, 33.33;—*criminal*, origin, 16.433a; *int.* asso., 33.147; *military*, 32.10; *Roman*, 149.672a
Law Review, Am. 32.74;—H., 33.367; W: w, 32.412
Lawns, winter, 47.690
Lawrence, W: B., 32.243
Leader, J. D. 33.200
Le Conte, J. 12.358*; *w* 32.-190
Lee, V. 32.33‖
Lefroy, 33.25, 367
Legends, w 33.117
Leiden univ., 62.491a
Leidy, J., 17.685a
Leigh, A., 32.267; 33.480
Leo XIII, 151.387a
Le Page *32.250; 48.283
Leslie. T. E. C., 18.101a
Lesseps [see Panama Canal] 33.25
Lessing, 47.159
Letournou, *w* 31.469
Letters, 151.445
Libel law, 33.315; suits, 32.-269, 463; 33.324, 350
Liberty statue, 33.504
Libraries, public, 33.448a; aids, 33.448a, 454; and publishers, 33.474; fiction in, 10.168a; 33.870a;—U. S. conference, 32.112a; Eng.—, 31.326; 33.314; Ital., 32.151
Lick obser., 33.430a
Liddell, G., 149.749
Lieber, F., 10.333a; *w* 32.189
Liebig, 3.232*; 9.49a
Life, human, 20.95a; statistics, ps. 10.697a; *professional:* bribery, 63.946; *social*, industrial ideal, 149.701; money, 61.922; discipline of poverty, 23.-310
Light, 16.517; houses, U. S., 33.346
Lillie, A., *w* 33.340; 48.840
Lincoln, A., mask, 23.223a*; pen, 33.112; R., 32.177
Lindau, P., 33.275, 316
Linde, A von der, *w* 32.221
Linton, E. L, 151.127**; *w* 32.411; W. J., q 32.204
Liquor question, 32.93; coffee-houses, 14.108; legislation (German), 32.165a; (N. Y.) 33.105; moral effect, 14.379a
Lisbon, 63.36a*
Liszt, q 33.494
Literature, [see American, etc. lit.] art, 47.730; sham admiration, 17.48a; autobiografy, 97.44a; biog., 48.-281; cont., 32.78a; *profession*, 97.423; authors, 7.93a (and editor), 62.789; reputations, 47.582; morality 97.119a; strain, 16.93a; style, 47.443; *study*, 1.396a
Littré, 32.407
"Livadia," 33.209
Liverpool, 33.243; plot, 33.107

Livingstone, D., 2.327a*; w 27.318; 32.63; 48.411; 62.-632
Livre, 32.75; 33.94
Lloyd, C., 62.164
Lobedanz, E., 32.184
Locke, w 31.396
Lockroy, E., *w* 33.497
Lockyer, J. N., 4.109*
Locomotion, 4.528a*; human, 6.48a*
Lodge, H: C., 28.110; 32.373; 48.415
Logarithms, w 32.149
London, 47.252a; archæ., w 32.352; press, 31.250a, 270a
Long, gov., 33.84
Long iland, early hist., w, 33.354; sound, 61.206a*
Longfellow, 31.212; *47.109
Longman, F. W.. *w* 32.376
Long Sault, 33.216
Loring, G: B., 32.360
Lorne, q., 33.327; and wife, 63.216*
Lotze, H., 33.95
Louis XI. 61.694*
Louisiana, hist., 31.370; 32.35
Lovejoy, E. P., w., 32.264
Lovell, S: w., 32.388
Lover, S: w., 31.259
Lowe, R. see Sherbrooke
Lowell mill girls, 48.593a; J. R., 62.252a*
Lowery, S: 33.241
Lowther, J., 32.53
Lubbock, q., 33.233
Lucas, J., 6.301
Lucretius, 18.333a; 47.58
Ludlow. T. W., q., 32.92; 33.413, 451
Lumby, J. R., 33.219
Luther, 61.38*; w 33.421
Luxury, 18.669a¶
Lydus, J., 149.672a
Lyell, sir C: 1.231*
Lying, invol., 14.611a
Lynedoch, ld., w. 31.361
Lyman, H. M., *w* 33.354
Lytton 1st, home, 28.9a*; 2d, 33.473; plagiarism, 47.136, 577
Maccabæus, w 32.356
McCalman, A. H. *w* 32.65
McCarthy, J. 63.669*
Macinghi, A. w 48.672**a
McClellan, w 33.200a
McCook, H: C., *w* 33,478
McCrary, q., 33.62, 92
McCrea, E. P., 33.305
McCulloch, J: *w* 47.368§§
McCurdy, J. F. q 32.405; *w* 33.458
Macdonald, F. 61.676a*; *G.* 33.54, 336; *J.* 31.313
Mac Dougal, P., 33.387
Macgeorge, *w* 32.376
Mac Gillivray, 31.341
McGrath, T. *w* 32.358
McIlvane, C. P., w 33.339
Mackensie, H. D. S., *w* 33.-358
Maclean, *K: S.* 32.98; *S: B.* 33.235, 350
McPherson statue, 33.65
Macquoid, K. S. *w* 33.479§
Mac Veagh, 32.177; 33.241, 366, 386, 404
"Madge", 33.146
Madison, J. 63.446*,*
Madrid, duke of, 33.45, 65
Magazin für die Lit., 33.-434
Magellan, str. 33.167
Mahaffy, *w* 31.294
Mahone, 31.298; 32.178, 195, 234; 33.281, 302
Main, D. M., *w* 32.262
Maine, *travels*, summering,

28.103; coast, 61.ii*; (W) 63.523a*; forest, 47.844a; *history*, 32.2, 19; 33.106, 226
Maintenon, *w* 32.368**a
Maistre, de, 47.67a
Malaria, 9.416a; 33.34, 374; w 33.366, 494
Malays, 33.443
Malherbe, 32.407*,*
Malley case, see Cramer
Mallock, 16.417; 33.79‡; 47.-65; 48.560‡
Malot, *w* 31.382¶
Mammoth cave, 33.374
Man, [see Babies, Sociology,] antiquity, 1.208a*; degeneracy, 1.482a; migrations, 1.290a; 16.322a¶; races, 19.289a*; (crossing,) 17.166a; (unity,) 1.61a; study, 1.327a
Manchester, earl, *w* 33.239
Manitoba, travels, 27.113a*
Manners, see Etiquet
Manzanillo, 33.407
Maps, 16.478a*
Marbles, ancient, ps 11.67a
Marcus Aurelius, ps 11.461a; 33.489, 510
Mario case, 33.509
Marlitt, 33.99
Marriage, 2.1a: 6.466a; prim. ps 10.272a; 17.203
Marsh, G: P. q, 32.88a; O. C., 13.612a*
Marshall, G: W. q 33.94
Martiis, *w* 33.222
Martin, st. 61.383; *H. N.* 32.-303; *W. A. P.* 32.245a
Martineau, H. 32.187; *J* 8.-129a
Martyn, H: 151.707
Marvin case, 33.167
Mary, st. w 33.200a
Maryland, hist., 32.350; 33.-493; records, 33.493
Mason, E. P. 10.585a
Massachusetts, *travels*, coast 23.49a; (W.) 61.873a*; 63.-643a*; *history*, colonial, 63.535a*; cont. 32.51; 33.-242, 244, 284; *militia*, 9th reg. 33.366; *politics*, city, 33.169a, 196
Mass. Ins. Technology, 23.-286a
Matches, ps 11.413a
Materialism, 3.645; 8.129a; 13.354a; 15.667a
Mathematics, teaching, 33.-273a
Mathews, W. S. B., 32.154;
Matthews. S., 32.67, 195, 251
Maudsley, 6.612*
Maurer, K., *w*, 31.342; 33.-238
Maxwell, J. C., 17.116*
May, T: P., *w* 33.336
Mayer, A. M., ps 10.230*; J. R. 15.397*
Mayor. J. B., 33.338
Mead, E. D., *w* 33.18
Measures, 19.652a
Meat, canned, 33.326
Medical prof'on, 2.422*,*a*; bibliog., 33.116; history, cont., ps 10-330a; 33.174, 5; laws regulating, 10.367a; (in N. Y.) 33.116; liability, 18.769a; quacks, 1.95a: study, 19.795a
Mediterranean canal, 33.445
Menstruation, w, 12.341
Meredith, G: *w* 31.411
Merimée, *w*, 32.202**a, 256a
Merrill, *G: E*, 33.454; 64.-149; *S*, 33.378; 48.832
Merv, 33.129, 367
Meslier, J: *w*, 14.241¶

Figures to the left of the period indicate the volume as follows: 1-9, 20-21, Popular Science; 10.11, International Review; 23, Century; 27.8, Lippincott's; 31.3, Nation; 47-8, Atlantic; 62-4, Harper; 97, Eclectic; 149-51, Living age.

Mesmerism, ps 11.12a
Mesnervi, 33.138a¶
Messolonghi, 33.367
Metalic arts exh., 33.478
Metcalfe, F., *w*, 31.324
Meteorology [see Storms, Weather Bureau], 15.684; 31.308; 33.233; *w* 33.335; yellow day, 63.948; infl. moon, ps 10.56a¶
Methodists [see Church] œc council, 33.209, 227, 245, 270
Metric system, 13.82a; 14.-757a
Metternich, *w*., 33.201**a
Metzu, G., 63.181*
Mexico, travels, 23.1a*; archæ., 32.94; lan., *w*., 32.61; railways, 33.367; 63.276a
Mexico, gulf, fish, 150.512
Michel, L., 31.439; 32.114; 33.45; *M*., 31.469
Michigan, travels, 28.321a*; fires, 33.208, 227, 264, 326, univ., 18.123; 32.168
Midhat, 33.25, 45, 65
Mieris, F., 63.184*
Milan, ind. exh., 32.369a
Milk, 28.416; use, 19.482a; condensed, 3.466
Mill, J: S., 3.367a*; 14.698a; 16.25a; 97.53**; infl., 62.-787
Miller, Joa., 33.274; M, 33.-435; W., 33.41, 44, 462; q 33.81
Millet, *F. D*., 32.229; J: F, w., 32.116
Millöcker, *w*, 33.375§§
Mills, *C*., 17.563; S. B., 62.-814*
Milner, G., *w* 33.440
Milton, 47.387
Milwaukee, 62.702a*
Mind [see Brain, Emotions] and disease, 6.562a; reading, ps 10.459a; ps. 11.362; overwork, 151.229
Mines, explosions, 15.200a; 33.485; ancient, 33.232; U. S., 27.86a
Minnesota finance, 32.197; 33.44, 84, 208, 226, 302, 304, 364; hist., 33.264, 284, 326
Miracles, 9.21a; modern, (Hammond) 10.225a; 12.-724; 32.132; 33.84
Mirzan case, 33.152
Mischief in middle age, 48.1a
Mississippi, hist., 31.386; 33.-106, 206, 386; land, 33.504
Miss. river, 33.346; jetties, w, 32.30
Mitchell, *A*., 31.467; 62.949; *S W*, 33.100; 47.284
Mivart, *w*, 32.393; 63.310
Möller, A., *w*, 32.260
Mohammedanism, hist., [see Califate] 150.707a; 151.-172a; lit., 33.138a; orders, 151.566a
Mohr, F., 17.402*
Molière 47.157
Molina, *w*, 32.61
Molinari, q, 31.265
Mollett, J: W., *w* 32.352
Mommsen sub., 31.439; *w* 32.6
Monaco, 33.85
Monastery, Baptist, 23.214a*
Monck, W. H. S., *w* 33.19
Money, (see Finance, Silver, etc.) rate interest, 11.22a
Mongredien, A, *w* 32.322
Monkeys, [see Apes,] 27.-544a*; 28.22a*, 380a
Monograph, 32.297
Monstrosities, human, 64.-105

Montagu, M. W. 10.549a
Montague, C: W., *w* 33.298
Monteil, *w* 33.298
Monumenta Germaniæ, 33.-492
Moody & Sankey, 33.387
Moon, ps 10.568a
Moore, C: H. *w* 33.93
Moose, 27.231a*
Morals, history, 16.267a; in beasts, 16.346a; and civilization, ps 11.549a
Morey letter, 31.297, 316a, 349, 352a, 385, 390a, 402
Morgan, D., w 33.519
Morgan, E. B. 33.305, 346; E. D. 33.326; L. H. 18.-114a*; 33.493
Morley, H: *w* 33.159; J: 64.-44*; S: q 33.344, 445
Mormons, 9.479a; ps 10.156a: 11.221a; 32.463, 467a; 33.-386, 405, 424, 502; hist. 63.-756a
Morocco, w, [trav.] 32.64
Morris, *C:* 32.46; *C,* §§31.-326; 32.18, 131; 47.365
Morse, E: S. 13.102*; S: F. B., 1.115*
Morton. L. P. 32.19; 33.107
Moscow fire, 33.265
Mott, L. 31.358
Mowbray, J: R. q 33.327
Mozart, 62.945
Mudford, W. H. 64.39*
Müller, F. M. q 33.176; *w* 23.150; 33.13
München, art study, 28.211
Mulford, E. *w* 48.699
Mulhall, M. G., w 31.331
Munger, T. T., *w* 23.154
Muntz, E. *w* 32.208; 33.-413¶
Murray, E. C. G., 33.505
MURRAY, 149.658‡
Murders, 33.45; U. S., 33.-62; (cal.) 32.214; *political* 48.780a; rht. asylum, 33.-148a; infernal machines, (*q. v.*) 33.63
Murdoch, J. E. *w*, 47.565
Museums, sci. Eur. ps 11.-472a
Music, 97.189a; w, 32.154a; 33.217; and elections, 33.-416; influence, 31.292; journals, 33.217; notation' 28.315;—in U. S. 63.947; Brooklyn, 33.495; England (fests) 33.275; Leipzig, 33.-488a: N. Y. 31.308, 326, 342, 359, 394, 410, 427, 445; 32.11, 27, 44, 75, 95, 114, 133, 150, 169, 186, 207, 244, 260, 298, 318, 335, 33.395, 416, 435, 454, 474, 513, 61.-144; 62.803a*; 63.304, 307; [opera] 33.317; 62.305; Norwegian, 33.513; oriental, 18.237a; Vienna, 32.-293a
Musical-Review, 33.217
Musset, 61.200*
Myer, A. J., 18.408a*
Myers, F. W. H., *w*, 32.153
Mykenai finds, 33.132a
Mythology, 18.43a; comp., 48.85a
Nadal, q, 32.56
Names, 33.198; 97.-355a: anatomical, 32.278; family, (U. S.) 32.114; accent, 47.299; (Indian,) 48.-716
Nantucket, 28.303a
Naples, bay, 149.812a
Napoléon III, 61.197; 151.57
Narcotics, 7.611a; 13.483a; 15.491a
Nation Index, 31.325

Natural history, curiosities, 64.97a*; study, 32.277;—Soc., (Boston) 32.334

Naumann, E., 31.330

Navies, w, 31.292; 32.66; 47.-423

Navagation, ocean, 3.717a

Navy, U. S., 33.346, 366, 385, 426

Needlework, art, 27.626; 61.655a

Negroes, U. S., 19.665a; 32.-236; exodus, 32.314; nos., 32.122, 185; soc. relations, 32.132

Nerves and morals, 2.416a

Netoleszha, q, 31.360

Neumarck, G: w, 33.338‡

Newark bank, 33.344, 346, 366

Newberry, J. S., 9.490*

Newcomb, S., ps 11.612*; 62.550*; *w*, 33.254

Newell, *C. M.* 33.336; *W. W.* 32.351¶

New England pesants, 27.418

Newfoundland, French claims, 32.113

New Guinea, 14.742a; 15.-57a; w 32.223a

New Jersey, courts, 33.104; hist. 33.106, 304

New London, 27.17a*

Newman, *mrs.* 33.336; rev., q, 33.22; J: H: 97.37a

New Mexico, travels, 61.-185a*

Newnham college, 97.134

New Orleans riot, 33.208, 227

Newport, 61.630; in Rev. 63.-463; casino, 63.944

New Testament, Mss. 33.-413; revision, 32.371a; 32.-380, 401a, 63.465, 472; 97.-223, 631a; 150.67a; in practice, 33.25, 68a

Newton, *C: T:* 31.449; 32.-137; *H:* 33.340

New Virginians, 32.248

New York city, w 33.134; 7th reg. *armory*, 32.390; *art*, [see Exhibitions.] 31.-309, 377, 445; museum, 61.-142; *casino*, 33.289a; *charities*, 32.68, 345; fresh air, 28.186a; *custom-house*. 32.104, 143; 33.84, 146; rules, 33.206; *Delmonico's* 33.191a; *education*, college, 13.106; schools, 16.695; [niht,] 17.-681; (trades) 23.286; *fires*, 33.285; dept, old, 62.191a* *harbor*, Montauk, 28.-425a*; immigration fees, 33.126, 128; pilots, 23.177a*; sharks, 33.106; *library*, free, 31.462; *park*, obelisk, 32.52; 61.792; *police* com., 32.231; *politics*, 31.281, 298, 315, 333, 337a, 419, 451, 454a; 32.2, 23a, 270; 33.82, 84, 146, 166, 186, 205, 224, 227, 244, 286a, 287a, 363; 63.147, 307; C. S. tenure, 33.154; election frauds, w 32.355a; *population*, Italian, 62.676a*; squatters, 61.562a*; working women, 61.25a*; *post-office*, 32.232; el. railways, 32.288, 308; 33.24, 44, 64, 84, 166, 185, 186, 262, 265, 285, 503; *society*, 62.624; new years, 32.1; *stock-exchange*, 33.407; *street* cleaning, 32.196, 198a, 231, 252, 269, 288, 309, 330a, 360, 379; *thea-*

Figures to the left of the period indicate the volume as follows: 1-9, 12-20, Popular Science; 10-11, International Review; 23, Century; 27-8, Lippincott's; 31-3, Nation; 74-8 Atlantic; 62-4, Harper; 97, Eclectic; 149-51, Living Age.

tres. 31.254, 446; 32.207; 33.227, 503; 47.362a; German, 33.375; *trade*, 33.108a; and . rys. 33.123; *water* supply, 33.326
N. Y. state, *code*, 32.169, 197, 217a; 33.184; *hist.* 31.-350, 370; 32.1, 19; 33.24, 44, 61, 64. 226, 244, 261, 264, 284, 304. 383, 388, 403; *taxation*, 32.36
Niagara, 1.564a*; 3.210a; 33.-170a, 215
Nicolay, J: G, *w*, 33.398
Nichol, J. *w*, 31.344
Nihilists, 10.ii; 32.253, 271, 289; 33.45, 119a, 167, 305, 347, 424, 427; 63.443
Niko, 33.303
Nohl, L: *w*, 32.192¶
No Name novels, 31.382; 32.303, 411; 48.564
Norris, W. E. 28.111; 33.-137
Norse lit. 33.513
North Carolina, hist. 32.308, 398; 33.103, 106, 125, 133a
Northcote, S. 32.367; q, 33.-263
Norton, C: E., 62.389*; *w* 27.-105; 31.345
Norway, w 33.334; travels, 47.770a; 48.39a, 366a, etc.; 63.882a*; women, 48.854
Norwood, 31.280
Nova Scotia, hist., 1710, 11.-493a; sport, 27.231a*
Noyes, gen., 33.195; C: J., 31.305; *S. B.* 32.73
Nubians, 17.512*
Numerals, ps. 10.736
Nursing, 9.173a; 27.521
Oakey, *miss* 63.632; *A. F.* 33.59; 63.792; *S. W.* 32.-181**
Oates, F. 33.439
Obeissances, 13.146a
Oberammergau play, (see Passion Plays,) actors, 33.-25
Oberhofen, 147.190
Obesity, 1.545a; 17.60a
Ocean messengers, 151.127
O'Connell, D. 61.204
O'Connor, T. P., q 33.302
Odes, 150.195a
O'Donnovan, 33.505
Odors, 6.142a
Odylism, ps 11.13
Offenbach, 10.286a; 31.254
Ohio, finance, 32.278; history, 33.106, 264, 304; w 31.325
Oil industry, U. S. 33.166; 47.320a
Old Testament, w 33.118a
Oliphant, *L.* 32.326; 63.468; *M. O. W.* 32.193‖; 33.99
Omens, 97.129
Oncken, W. 31.425; 32.168
Opera, [see Music] w 33.-101; bouffe, 31.275
Opium, 12.555
Opossums, 8.149a*
Orange, W: of, 62.493*
Ordeals, 9.307a
Oregon war bonds, 32.251
O'Reilly, J. B. 62.397*; *w*, 47.859
Oriental Soc., U. S. 31.326; 33.275
Orientals, 3.493
Ornament, evo. in, 6.266a
Orpheon societies, 33.275
Oscar I., 64.13*; II., 64.1*
Ostade, A. van, 61.899a*
Oswald, F. L. · 27.110; 33.-228§
Otis, C. P., *w*, 33.182
Ouida, 32.173; 33.394
Owls, ps 11.143a*

Oxenford, J: 63.845*
Oybin, 150.351
Oysters, 6.1a; beds, 20.29a; 27.479
Pacific states, archæ, ps 10.353a; ry. discrimination, 33.113a
Paddock, A. G., *w*, 33.137
Päli text soc., 33.117
Pailleron, E: *w*, 33.449a
Pain, fysical uses, 27.302a
Paine, T: 18.563
Painting, (see Art) color blindness, 1.174a
Palæontology, 16.219a; 17.350a; 20.165a
Palatine Notebook, 33.51
Palfrey, J: G., 32.318
Pall Mall Gazette, 31 250
Palmer family, 33.33; *E: H.* 32.62; F. A. 33.504
Palustre, *w*, 32.280; 47.866
Panama, 33.367; canal, 16.840a, 842a; 31.434; co., 33.827; and U. S., 20.273; 33.326, 327, 347, 348a, 367, 384, 441, 445, 481, 484, 485
Pancrates, 33.51
Panizzi, w, 32.62; 33.275
Papacy, hist. 33.45, 127, 303, 305, 505; income, 97.718
Paper, taxation, 33.135
Paralysis, 15.40a
Paris *art* schools, 23.259a*; 27.269a; life, 28.435a; models, 28 522; école des *sciences politiques*, 31.378; *life*, 28.571a; *politics*, 32.57a
Parker, F. J. 31.261‖
Parliaments, [see England, etc.] procedure, 32.87a
Parnell, 32.123, 161; 33.265, 285, 303, 305, 347; 62.307
Parr, 32.16‡
Parry, B. 31.269
Parsons murder, 33.465; W. 28.186
Parton, J. q 33.292; *w* 23.151; 33.276; 48.260a; 63.473; 97.474a
Pascal, 31.251
Passion plays, w 32.29; Ammergau, 61.472; in N. Y., 31.386
Passions, see Emotions
Pasteur, 151.323a
Paston, 151.135**
Patent law, 15.612a
Patriotism, 2.708a
Patterson, C. P., 33.128; R., 33.106
Patti, A., 33.387, 395
Pauperism and hospitals, 9.738a
Pavements, 7.80a; 23.154
Peabody bequest, 33.327; museum, 33.232; 63.670a*
Peace society, 33.347
Pearce, J. A. q 32.239
Peard, 31.382; 47.711
Peirce, B., 18.691a*; 31.268a; 33.452
Pekin, college, 31.326
Pemberton, J. C. 33.45
Penazzi, L. 33.115
Penn, W: grave, 33.64, 105; 64.83a*; 150.637; pictures, 62.1a*
Pennsylvania, travels, [E] 23.209a*; 64.88a; coal, 33.116; history, 32.105; 33.205, 261, 264, 282, 383, 403, 504
Pensions, U. S. 33.363, 426; office, 28.200a; 33.44, 281, 301
Pepys, 150.408a; w 31.417
Perinchief, O., w, 16.561
Perry, *N*, 33.98; 47.284; S: 31.350

Figures to the left of the period indicate the volume as follows: 1-9, 12-20, Popular Science; 10-11, International Review; 23, Century; 27-8, Lippincott's; 31-3, Nation; 47-8, Atlantic; 62-4, Harper; 97, Eclectic; 149-51, Living Age.

Persecution, 32.10

Peru, *archae.*, w 32.137a; 33.33; *art.* anc. 33.374; *history*, 32.53; 33.45, 85, 167, 209, 245, 305, 325, 327, 364, 367, 384, 425, 427, 485; and U. S., 33.390, 405, 441; Co., 33.484, 486a

Perugino, 150.149

Pessimism, ps 11.682a

Petermann, A: H: 14.231*

Petroleum, 9.140a; German, 33.147

Pettenkofer, q 33.295

Pewter, old. 48.846

Ph. . . . see F. . . . .

Phear, J: B. 32.228

Phelps, Dodge case, 31.419; *A.* 33.438; W: W. 33.265

Philadelphia, history, 31.334, 339; 32.122, 148; 33.426; frauds, 33.445

Phillips, solic. 32.359; W, q 33.365; 63.625; W. H., q, 33.114

Phoinikians, 47.375

Pianos, ps 11.691a; 33.416

Piatt, J. J. 32.319

Picture buying, 27.104; framing and hanging, 63.552*

Pierce case, 33.347; *E. L.* 32.246a

Pierson, H. W. 33.359

Pikes in civil war, 32.259; W: B., 63.260

Pinchard, 151.509

Pinto, S., 33.74; *w* 28.213; 33.53; 48.835; 63.791

Pittsburg, 62.49a*

Pius-Verein, 31.286a

Plagiarism, cases, 31.411; 33.491

Plaisted, gov., q, 32.84

Plants, 97.500a; history, w, 31.342; climing, 17.635a; and liht, 33.272

Platt, T: C. 32.35, 38a, 51, 397; 33.2, q, 205

Plowed Under, 32.228

Plutarch, *w* 31.395‖¶; 33.415¶

Poe, E. A. 47.523; 61.788; w 10.26a; 31.360; *w* 31.408

Poetry, 33.197; morality, 149.731a; theories, 150.682a

Poets' wives, 47.iv

Police types, 33.88a

Political Economy, 16.601a; w, 32 212; in U. S., ps 10.366; Germany, 31.409; payt. pub. dets., 11.246a; produce and consumption, ps 11.306a

Political Education soc., 31.342

Politics [see Institutions, Parliaments,] 3.172a; ceremony, 12.385a; discipline, 2.129a; gifts, 13.25a; international, infl. telegraf, 19.101a; lit. men, 61.143; military system, 19.750a; monarchy, 15.545a; nat. morality, 61.788; parties, ps 11.734a; stupidity of politicians, 12.163a; primitive, 18.1a; rihts, 11.152a

Pollock, F. 32.376

Poncas, 32.3, 67, 83, 90, 103, 125a. 141, 159

Ponies, wild, 28.476

Poole, D. C. 33.320; *R. L.* 31.366

Poor, L. E. 32.66

Porcelain, painting, 61.903a; old, 33.94

Pork, disease, 32.186; trade, 33.427, 435, 445

Porpoises, 149.638*,*

Figures to the left of the period indicate the volume as follows: 1-9, 12-20, Popular Science; 10-11, International Review; 23, Century; 27-8, Lippincott's; 31-3, Nation; 47-8, Atlantic; 62-4, Harper; 97, Eclectic; 149-51, Living Age.

Porter, F. J: 31.420, 435
Portfolio, 31.341; 33.34
Portland, duke of, 151.758
Portraits, composit, 13.461a*; generic, 15.532a
Portugal, *travels*, 63.iii; w 31.343; *history*, 33.387
Post-Office, *U. S.* [see Star-routes,] 32.290a; 33.285, 326, 346, 406, 452; forein, 32.104; rules, 33.404; *English*, 151.636; w 32.138; parcels, 149.704; *Swiss*, orders, 33.444
Potter, O. B. 33.332; q 32.240
Pottery, 4.59a*; U. S. 62.-357a*; Cincinnati, 62.834a*
Pourtales, 18.549*
Powell, B. q, 33.243
Power, new, 32.318; wasted, 15.289a
Poynter, E. J. 31.365; 33.9, 99
Praxitelês, w 32.75
Preece, W. H. q 31.463
Pregnancy, ps. 10.38a
Presbyterian council, 31.245
Preston, W: C. 11.354
Prince, J. C. 149.752
Princeton college, 18.122
Priestley, J. 6.90a
Prisons, 10.306a; 11.234a; 97.316a
Private Sec. 28.527; 33.-436
Proctor, R: A. 4.486*; *w* 32.-191
Prolfs, R., 33.376
Profesy, 3.732a
Progress, 18.553
Prohibition in N. C. 32.308, 133a: 33.104
Protoplasm, 8.67a¶; ps 11.-422a; 15.729a
Proverbs, 151.699; Scotch, w 32.221; Sicilian, 31.411
Providence ly. lists, 32.277
Prussia, *admin.*, cities, 33.-353; volkswirthschaftsrath 32.128; *hist.* 33.305
Pullan, R. P., 31.440
Pulling, F. S., 32.185
Pulman car co., 33.505
Pumpelly, 33.193
Punch, 97.558a
Punishment [see Prisons] 33.414; w, 33.37
Puritans, U. S., 61.947
Pyle, H., *w*, 33.496
Quackenbos, G. P., 33.65
Quakers, U. S., 47.440; in N. E., 32.259; 33.330a, 372a, 412a
Qualtrough, 33.122
Quilter, 33.9
Quincy, Ill., floods, 33.326, 346
Quinet, w, 33.176a
Quotations. hist., 63.787
Rabelais, 61.820a*
Racine, 47.158
Racinet, 31.309; 32.298
Rae, W. F., q, 32.183; *w*, 33.320
Rafaelle, w, 32.208
Railways, 32.322; accidents, 16.414; 33.128; beautifying, 33.334; ship, 63.905a*; U. S., 32.160, 199a, 203a, 273a, 333, 386; 47.317a; law, 32.246a; prices and courts, 33.82, 92a; robberies, 33.42, 44, 206, 208, 245, 265, 285,; stock-watering, 32.241a, 254a, 258, 273, 276a, 294a; war, 33.106, 128, 130a, 146, 243, 326, 506a
Ralegh, 151.603a
Randall, q, 33.345
Randazzo, 33.227, 243, 245,

Figures to the left of the period indicate the volume as follows: 1-9, 12.20, Popular Science; 10-11, International Review; 23, Century; 27-8, Lippincott's; 31-3, Nation; 47-8, Atlantic; 62-4, Harper; 97, Eclectic; 149-51, Living Age.

264, 266a, 283, 285, 344, 346, 445, 503
Ranke, 31.424
Rankin, M., 33 274, 315; W. J. M., 12.236*
Rats, 4.344a*
Raum, q, 33.226
Rawlinson, G., 33.118, 155a
Raymond, J: H., w, 32.356
Reading, 8.212a; w, 31.274; ry., 32.1, 21
Rebello, see Randazzo
Récamier, 32.89; 48.137
Réclus, *w*, 33.142; 63.309
Recreation, 14.780a; 15.772a; 16.640a; 19.450; summer, 28.209
Redell, M. C., q, 33.404
Redfield, H. V., 31.465
Redhouse, J. W., 33.138¶a
Reformation, 149.653
Reed, *E. J.*, 32.281; T: B., 33.367
Reference index, 32.205
Regnault, 23.15a
Reichenbach, *w*, 33.99
Rein, J. J., *w*, 33.317
Religion, 47.68; 151.763a; and epilepsy, 2.605a; God, 48.532a; origin, 97.86a, 858a; 150.131a; primitive, 15.795a; 16.56a; science of, 32.407
Religions, revue des, 33.494
Remenyi, 62.817*
"Remus," see Harris, J. C.
Rémusat, 33.110**
RENAN, ps11.216‖; *w*, 31.271; 33.389a; 32.198
Renouf, 47.130
Rent, 33.365
Repub. league, 32.326
Reumont, 32.321
Rhein, songs, 61.201
Rhode Island, name, 33.74, 92
Ricasoli, B., 11.268a
Richardson, A. S., 150.214a
Richmond, duke, 32.367
Richter, 33.427
Rideing, W. H., 32.351
Ridings, E., 149.749
Riggs, G. W., 33.167
Ripley, G., 61.633
Risano, 150.824
Ritchie, A. T., 33.137
Ritter, C: 16.689a*
Roach, q, 33.447
Robbins, D. C., q, 33.104
Robertson, col. 32.214, 216a, 231, 253, 272a, 325; 33.81
Robeson, q, 33.183
Robinson, J. R., 63.667*; W: 33.420
Rocca, della, 32.64
Rochambeau papers, 32.3
Rochefort, 32.3; 33.265; *w*, 32.410
Rochester obser., 31.325
Roe, E. P., 31.382
Rogerson, J. B., 149.749
Rogers, J. E. T., q, 31.371; *w*, 33.360; *W: B.*, 9.606*
Rome, ANCIENT, aqueducts, 32.147a; con. w, 33.494; sanitory arrangements, 32.221; society, 149.647; *later empire*, w, 32.29; MODERN, campagna drainage, 151.505a; art study, 27.1a*; malaria, 151.639; Americans in, 27.617a; riot, 150.639
Rood, 16.274
Rosas, 61.205*
Rose, R., 149.753
Rosenthal, I., 33.19¶
Rosmini, 151.771a
Ross, D. W., 31.341; 32.260
Rossa, O., q, 33.143
Rosse, 33.354

Figures to the left of the period indicate the volume as follows: 1-9, 12-20, Popular Science; 10-11, International Review; 23, Century; 27-8, Lippincott's; 31-3, Nation; 47-8 Atlantic; 62-4, Harper; 97, Eclectic; 149-51, Living Age.

Rossetti, C. G., 97.708
Rossini, w, 33.140; *w*, 33.-375; *miss*, 33.454
Roubaud, 33.332
Rouher, 33.107
Roumania, forein relations, 33.445, 465
Round, W. F. R., *w*, 33.98
Round Robin novels, 32.-411; 33.54, 99, 337, 436
Rousseau, 97.47**
Roustan, 33.485
Roy, T. B., *w*, 31.341
Royal Society, 6.655a
Royet, O., *w*, 32.279
Rubber, see Caoutchouc
Rubbish, 16.97
Rubinstein, *w*, 31.394; 33.-90a; 435
Rugby, Tenn., 31.246; 33.127, 288; 62.147; w, 33.59
Ruggles, S. B., 33.107
Rumford, 9.231*
Rummel, F., 62.813*
Ruskin, 33.220a
Russell, *C:* 32.188; *W. C.*, 32.17; W: G., 33.504; W: H., 63.846*; *W. S.*, 47.445
Russia, *travels*, 151.183a; *courts*, 33.445; *finance*, 33.407; *forein relations*, extradition, 33.305; Germany, 33.207; *history*, 32.-177, 233, 399, 361; 33.63, 127, 167, 187, 305, 327, 367, 387, 485; w, 33.16; *society*, country, 27.252a
Rutherford, w, 28.631; 32.-392**
Ryssakoff, 32.271
Sabine, sir E: 2.238
Sadi, 32.339¶
Sahara, flooding, 8.665a; ry., 32.318; wells, 16.530a
Saint Beuve, index, 33.274
St. Lawrence, 27.529a*; camping, 150.767; canals, 63.415a; 1000 iles, 63.501a*
St. Louis pol. 32.252
Saintsbury, G: 31.468; 32.-337
St. Simon, w, 31.366
St. Victor, P. de, 33.25; *w*, 47.288
Sala, G: A. 64.36*
Salisbury, marquis of, 32.-367; cathedral, 62.650a*
Salmagundi club, 31.445
Salmon, 19.1a
Salt, 1.405a; ind., U. S. 33.-154
Salvini, 23.110a
Salzburg conf., 33.295
Sanders, D. 33.115
San Francisco, Chinese, 27.-123a*; 62.70a*; vigilance com. 11.78a
Sanscrit, w, 32.152; 33.10; *lit.* 31.359¶; 33.275; study, 32.261
Saratoga springs, 19.24a
Sardou, A. 33.332; *V*, 31.-377; 47.369§§¶
Sargent, E. 32.395
Sauveur, 33.153
Savage, M. J. 17.565
Savannah riot, 33.245
Sayce, A. H. 23.148; 32.95
Scandinavia, archæ. 33.380; lit. w, 32.95
Scenery and imag., 151.383
Scent, 17.359a
Schäffer, C: q, 33.215
Schell, 31.281
Scherr, J: *w*, 32.157¶
Schiller, 47.163; *w*, 149.657; 151.823**
Schleswig, coast, 28.228a*
Schliemann, 27.316; 32.96a; 62.630; 150.771a

Figures to the left of the period indicate the volume as follows: 1-9, 12-20, Popular Science; 10-11, International Review; 23, Century; 27-8, Lippincott's; 31-3, Nation; 47-8, Atlantic; 62-4, Harper; 97, Eclectic; 149-51, Living Age.

Schlözer, 33.185, 290
Schönhof, J., *w*, 33.376
Schofield, q, 31.349
School Herald, 32.168
Schools, U. S., ps 11.713*⁎*; 16.663a; supervision [Adams] 61.984a
Schopenhauer, infl., 31.447a; *w*, 28.317¶; 33.158¶
Schouler, J., *w*, 10.495‖
Schubert, w, 33.140; *w*, 33.295, 354, 474
Schumann, R, 32.18¶; 33.495
Schurz, 10.380a; 31.279; 32.3, 125a, 159, 178, 196; q, 31.245, 280
Schütt, O, *w*, 33.198§
Schwatka, w, 33.420
Science, 1.697a; 2.93a; 3.105a; *dred of*, 13.411a; *history*, 8.385a; 13.257a¶; anc. 9.438a¶; martys of, 17.71a; early Eng., 17.669a; cont., 33.233; 151.195a; German, 8.369; *and lit.* 15.166a; *religion*, 2.79a; 6.227a, 362, 599a; 7.66a; 8.434a; 9.690a; ps 10.72a; ps, 11.367, 620; 12.1a: 14.621a; immortality 1.26a; *study*, 1.451a: *use*, 2.641a; 7.354a
Science, Am. Asso., 33.115, 136; Brit.—33.269
Science, 33.93; *Primers*, 17.269
Scotch Sermons, 18.559
Scotland, land q, 33.262, 265. 285, 443, 445
Scott, C. 32.463; 64.38*; *L*, 32.185; W, mother, 150.317; W. S. 47.664
Scoville, G: 32.464; q, 33.483, 485
Scribe, 47.678a
Scribner's Magazine, 23.160a; *31.426
Scrofula 19.599
Scudder, *H. E.*, 31.346; 47.280; *S: H.*, 32.150; 33.339
Seabury, S: 10.314a
Sealsfield, C: 31.342
Searle, W. S., 33.100
Secchi, P. A., 12.742*
Sekles, S., *w*, 31.331
Sellar, W. Y., *w*, 33.140
Semites, w, 33.355
Semler, H: q, 33.414
Sen, K. C., 31.464
Senate officers, 32.195, 213, 234a, 251, 270, 287, 325, 344a; 33.226
SENIOR, N. W., 151.48**a
Sense, evo. of new, 16.66a
Sensier, A., 32.116
Sergeant, L., 31.251
Servetus, 12.91a*
Servia & Austria, 33.305
Sessions, *F. C.*, 32.305§; L. B., 33.24, 166, 227
Sevigné, w, 33.381
Seward, G: F: 32.134; 62.951
Sewell, gen., 32.51
Sewerage, 18.806a
Sewing machines, use, ps 11.481a
Sex [see Women] differences, 20.184a; genesis, 16.167a
Shakspere, 47.383; w, 27.419; 32.135; 33.438; Bacon theory, 32.219; *w*, (Salvini) 23.117a; 47.302§§; 149.653; ballads illustrating, 63.52a*; provincialisms, 48.850; rimes, 47.438, 581; Hamlet, 48.467a; Iago, 48.203a, 421
Shaler. N. S., 33.39

Sharks, ps 10.348a
Sharpe, 32.2
Sheep-shooting, 151.535a; mt. 27.342a*
Shelley, 47.521; *w*, 47.441
Sherbrooke, lord, q, 31.351
Sherman, J: 31.280**, 298, 369, 335, 33.366; q, 32.251; I., 32.61; W: T., q, 32.10
Shervashidze, 33.445
Shetland iles, trav., 151.155a
Shipbilding, anc., 151.572
Shipping, *U. S.*, 10.184a; 31.264; 32.106a, 129a; 33.-404, 447a, 466a, 471, 491; 47.166a; *French*, 32.349; *German*, 32.349
Shipton, mother, 64.102*; w, 33.141
Shirlaw, W., 47.295
Shirner, E: J. q, 32.314
Shooting, 27.231a*; 61.870a*; 63.823a*; 151.535a
Shore, H: N., 32.139
Sibley, J. L., 33.58
Sicilian legends, w, 33.118
Siemens, q, 33.272
Signal service, see Weather Bureau.
Signorelli, *w*, 31.329
Silk culture, Burma, 151.253; mfg., U. S., 16.419; trade, Japan, 33.427
Silliman, B., 16.550a*
Silver question, 97.8a; U. S., 31.266a, 370, 401, 434, 452; 32.123, 163a, 179, 195, 233, 270, 271, 288, 3.10a, 326, 343; 33.22, 25, 27a, 44, 71, 183, 423, 505
Simmons, J. F., *w*, 32.319
Sitting Bull, 33.65, 344
Slavery and Jews, 149.707; U. S. 11.409; struggle, w, 32.264, 280a
Sleep [see Dreams,] 1.411a; 19.334
Sloths. 27.436a*
Small pox, 151.329a
Smith college, 33.493; C: P, 33.128; *E:* 33.381; G, 32.-399; q, 32.148; 33.325, 445; *w*, 16.267; 23.148; 32.184; H. B. w, 31.381; J. L. 6.-238*; J. R: q, 32.243; R, 31.350; 32.381; *w*, 19.413; S. I. q, 33.450; W. H., 63.-853*; *W. R.* 63.473
Smithsonian Ins., 33.232
Smyth, J. F. 33.44; *W: H.* 33.76
Snakes, 4.257a*; charming, 15.606a, 841
Snelling, W: J. 33.373
Soap bubbles, 9.575a
Socialism, 14.389, 577a; *agitation*, 33.45, 147; U. S., 33.233; German, 48.801a; [govt.] 32.128, 348a
Social Science, 1.159a; Am. asso., 33.208
Social Subjects, frendship, 151.125; decayed gentility, 63.788; hobbies, 149.698; mrs. Grundy, 61.304; over-estimated peple, 150.756; stupid—, 47.587; admiration, 151.822
Society, 9.1a; dinners, 27.206; industrial, 20.1a; romance modern life, 48.640a
Sociology, 1.vii; 47.75a; w, 31,467a, 469
Soil, w, 33.295
Solomon, w, 33.94
Songs, collec, 32.11; 33.334
Sophoklês, *w*, 32.48¶; at Harvard, 23.65a*, 32.347a, 364a; 48.10a; 63.464
Sothern, 62.790

Figures to the left of the period indicate the volume as follows: 1-9, 12-20, Popular Science; 10-11, International Review; 23, Century; 27-8, Lippincott's; 31-3, Nation; 47-8 Atlantic; 62-4, Harper; 97, Eclectic; 149-51, Living Age.

Soudan, 32.318
South Carolina, census, 31.264, 370; 32.83; duels, 31.452; 32.37; 33.164; negroes, 32.37
Southern States, w, 33.234a; *travels*, 61.165a*; *agric.*, 11.349; census, 10.439a; 32.37; *education*, 11.309a, 405; 32.309; *history*, 10.197a; 31.297, 316, 318a, 322a, 333, 339a, 356a; 32.240, 257a; 33.461; 47.391a; 63.784; *society*, 28.205a; before war, 11.405a; carpet-baggers, 31.316; homicide, 31.463, 465; 32.287; small towns, 47.648a
Southey, w, 61.146
Spain, *travels*, 28.334 etc.*; *church*, 33.85; *finance*, 33.327; *history*, moorish dominion, 27.425a*; 1808-14, 31.362; cont., 11.209a; 32.85, 96; 33.129, 147, 167, 209, 245, 305, 367, 387, 427, 445; 150.348; *railways*, 33.285
***Sparhawk, F.* 32.302; 47.861**
Sparrows, 15.412
Speculation, ps. 10.371
Speech, [see Deaf-Mutes] infirmities, 7.463a; tungless, 3.627a
Speir, G. M. 32.269; 33.166
Spelling Reform, [see English language,] 32.28; 33.176
***Spencer, H.* 6.20a*; 8.235a, 620; 9.243¶; 11.60; 15.705; 16.409a; 17.795a; 19.846a; 31.344; 32.24a; 47.77, 881**
Spenser, 47.382
Spiders, 1.674a*
Spielhagen, q, 31.327; *w*, 31.313; 32.302; 33.235
Spies, 16.122
Spinoza, ps 11.216a¶
Spiritism, ps 11.12a, 750; 12.745; 15.577a¶, 700; w, 48.417; mediæval, 16.354a
***Spofford, A. R.* 32.219; *H. P.* 32.229**
Sponges, 3.529a*
Sottiswoode, w: 14.105*
Sprague estate, 33.106
Spring, 47.764a; 61.65a*; P. B. q, 33.298
***Springer, R. R.*, 32.227**
Spurzheim, 32.174
Squid, 28.124a*
Stacke, L., *w*, 33.355, 472
Stael, mrs. de 27.62a; 150.515a
Stage, 27.522; w, 33.298; actors, 97.337a; applause, 48.280; authors, 33.274; gestures, 97.624a; French, w, 32.220‖
Stamps, hand, 23.157
Stanley, A. P., 33.45, 51, 65, 150a, 302, 445, 465, 547a; 63.911a*; 97.593a; 151.3a
Star routes, 32.287, 307, 314, 325, 360, 464; 33.61, 262, 264, 285, 304, 364, 366, 384, 386, 406, 426, 444, 464, 484, 504
Statham, 33.346, 343
Statius, *w*, 149.771a
Steamers, accidents, 33.23, 166, 146, 187, 203, 262, 327, 346, 347, 366; large, 33.326; *U. S.* 33.504; taxation, 32.463; forein, 33.465
***Stearns, W. A.*, 33.203; 64.153**
Steel industry, U. S., 19.808a; 32.296, 350, 404a; German,

33.265
Steen, J. 61.852*
Stephens, F. 32.185
Stern, S. M. 33.376
Sternberg, C. 31.291
Sterne, S., q, 31.350
Steuben, 33.304; family, 33.-291
Stevens Ins., 23.287; *A* 32.-228‖; *C: W.*, 33.18; H. 32.-389
Stewart, A. T. body, 33.146; B., ps 11.359*
Stickney, A. q 33.74; *w*, 18.-129; 33.153
Stigand, 32.220
Stillman, W. J. 32.278; q 32.132, 316a
Stirling, E. 32.267
Stock-market, 33.210a
Stockholm ly. pubs., 31.292
Stockton, F. R. 33.477
Stöckhardt, J. A. 19.261*
Stokes, G: G. 7.742*
Stokley, W. S., 32.123
Stone, age. 2.343a*
Storm, J. 32.220
Stoughton, W: 32.119
Stoves, 16.124
Stowe. E. 33.9
Strahan, E.. 33.496
Stratford de Redcliffe, 150.-170a; 151.348**a
Strikes, Eng., 33.367
Struve, O. W: 17.263*
Stuart, C. E. 61.678*; "descendants," 150.768
Stuart, G. 10.64a
Stuttgart, Am. library, 32.-276
Sudan, 33.218a
Sugar, La., 11.597a; maple, 62.641a*
Suicide, 8.88a; 16.798; w, 33.-517a; and religion, 20.220a
Sullivan, A. M., q, 33.325; *A.* S. 62.809*
Sully, J: 33.457
Summer in poetry, 150.757
Sun, eclipse, w, 32.171a; rays, 32.89
Sunday observance, 9.365a; 18.246a; 47.526a
Sunderland ly. 33.215
Sunstroke, 19.171
Superstition, 6.513a: 12.-232; 15.268**; 64.97a*; w, 33.221
Surgery, 28.595a; 33.434
Suricates, 16.318a*
Swallows, 7.315a
Swarthmore col. 33.245, 294
Sweden, *travels*, ps 10.450a; *royal fam.* 64.1a; *lit.* w, 33.153
Swinburne, *w*, 32.98; 47.856
Swindles, 62.788
Switzerland, agric. 62.685a*; 147.190; criminals, 33.327, 465; *history*, cont. 33.129, 347, 445; future, 31.395
Sword, 97.145a; 149.707a
Sylt, 28.228a*
Symonds, 31.311†; 61.308
Syria, w, (travels) 32.336; 33.378; Jews in, 151.631
Tacitus, ed., 31.260
Tagliche Rundschau, 33.332
Tahoe, lake, 20.225
Taine, 33.198; 63.950
Tait 32.24a
Talleyrand, 32.386**; 63.-629**
Talmage, 31.435, 452
Tammany, 32.270
Tangier, 63.ii*
Tanner case, 61.792
Tarif, U. S., 10 131a; 31.267a, 279, 283a, 454; 32.93; 33.-

Figures to the left of the period indicate the volume as follows: 1-9, 12-20, Popular Science; 10-11, International Review; 23, Century; 27-8, Lippincott's; 31-3, Nation; 47-8, Atlantic; 62-4, Harper; 97, Eclectic; 149-51, Living Age.

205, 247a, 344, 345, 428a, 501; conf., 33.383, 403, 406, 442
Taswell-Langmead, 33.331
Tauchnitz, 47.141
Taxation, theory, 33.67; *U. S.*, evasion, 48.285; interstate commerce, 10.428a; personal, 32.86a
Taylor, baron, 33.393; H.. 33.369; Z, 47.234a
Tchaikoffsky, 33.395
Tchernyshevski, 33.120
Tchihatchef, 31.259
Teaching, w, 32.340
Tearle, O., 47.362
Tehauntepec canal, 63.905a
Telefone, invention, 33.366; Eng. decision, 31.452
Telegraf, 63.705a; subterranean, 33.265; U. S., [see W. U.] consol., 32.55a, 84; and courts, 31.434;—govt., 19.-400a
Temperaments, 12.306a
Templars, hist., w, 31.428
Tennessee finance, 32.253
Tennis, 150.734a; w, 33.473; costume, 28.521
Tennyson, 10.178a; 31.430; 47.425; 150.451a
Teredo, 13.400a*
Thackeray, A.. I., [see Ritchie, A.. T] W: M., 32.-56a; *_**47.133, 725; *w*, 97.-96†a
Thames, 62.211a*
Thayer, A., q, 33.368, 388, 431
Theatre français, 33.351
Theology, 3.340a
Thomas, G: H., w, 32.338; T., 31.275; 62.803*
Thompson, J: q, 33.125; *L. O.*, 33.400; *S. D.*, 32.45, 192
THOMS, W: H., 97.489**a; 151.813**
Thomson, *J.*, 33.156a; 48.839; sir W: ps 10.357*
Thoreau, 32.322; 64.152
Thornet, 32.16
Thornton, sir E: 33.24
Thüringen, travels, 61.38a*; soc., 150.371
Thugs, 33.442
Thurber, F. B., q, 32.203, 241, 276; 33.166
Three Americas ry., 33.47a
Thunder showers, 7.340a
Thursby, E. C., 62.817*
Tichborne claimant, 33.62
*Tidemand**, 33.334
Tilden, q, 33.284
Tilton, J. R., 47.290*
Timayenis, T. T., *w*, 32.339
Timber, 2.582a; dry rot, 15.-525a
Tune, reckoning, 11.179a; standard, ps 11.174; 32.317, 332; 48.710
Times, 63.839a
Tincker, M.. A., 27.631; 32.-410; 47.860
Tingle, q, 33.423
Tissot, V., 33.119, 137
Titles, hist., 14.17a
Toadstools. 7.129a; ps 11.93a
Tobacco cult., U. S., 33.10; taxation, Germany, 33.212a; use. 2.167; 6.76a; (women) 33.275
Toedt, 32.11
Toland, M. B. M., *w*, 32.98
Tomes, R, 33.59**; 61.949**
Tompson, B., 33.116
Tools, ps 10.173a*
Tornöe, *w*, 33.276
Torrey, J: 3.63a*
Tourgee, q, 32.196; *w*, 31.-347; 32.314; 47.120

Figures to the left of the period indicate the volume as follows: 1-9, 20-21, Popular Science; 10.11, International Review; 23, Century; 27.8, Lippincott's; 31.3, Nation; 47-8, Atlantic; 62.4, Harper; 97, Eclectic; 149-51, Living age.

IRISTIAN UNION.

AN ABBOTT, EDITOR.

st of January, 1882, The Christian
upon its thirteenth year and twenty-
In the future, as in the past, it Pro-

I.—HELPFUL.

every week something which will
ers to be more true, more patient,
ous, more gentle, more faithful—in a
Christian men and women. It will
to be forbearing, children to be obe-
nts to be hearty, employers to be con-
ghbors to be friendly, and friends to
It will help every heart to bear its
, and a neighbor's burden too, and to
near to God by a daily life more worthy
ristian manhood.

33.206
Tuckey, J.. 31.278‖
Tufts, W. W., q. 33.293
Tunis, history, 150.308a; French in, 32.253, 289, 309, 311a, 313, 363a; 33.45, 46a, 63, 65, 70a, 85, 107, 185, 187, 209, 227, 228a, 245, 265; 33.262, 285, 305, 327, 347, 366, 387, 407, 427, 445, 465, 474, 483, 485; 150.349; and England, 32.402a
TURGENIEV, 97.440; 150.692a
Turkey [see Mohammedanism], w, 32.338; *travels* med., 32.211a; *finance*, 31.335; 33.327, 347, 425; *forein relations*, Austria, 150.349; *history*, w, 33.240; cont., 31.247, 265, 281, 320a, 387; 33.407; 61.745a; attentats, 33.167; murders, 31.335; *post-office*, 33.445; *society*, 62.603a
Turner, *w**, 32.8; C: T., 32.8
Turpin, 32 408
Tuson, R: V., 15.129
Twain, 40.843
Twins, 8.345a
Tyfoid, 14.514a; 16.460a
Tyler, K. E., 28.632; 33.455; *M. C.*, 33.373
Tylor, E. B., 33.181
Tyndall, 1.751; 2.103a*; 6.500; *w*, 8.489; 11.63; fund, 32.316
Tyner, 33.301, 324, 326, 336
Type-writer, 23.155
Typografy, 33.174
U*nderwood, A. B.* 32.32
Undset, I. 32.93
Union League decoration, 32.169;—Pacific monopoly, 33.113
iversal ins. co., 33:44
ersities, *U.S.* 33.173; 61.-
; 62.627; comp. attend-
3.235a; degrees, 32.-
ance, 33.2; [endow-
11.258a; [expen-
govt. (self) 10.-
, 697; gradu-
n,) 11.114a;
556a; ora-
ience, 7.-
10.313a;

Figures to the left of the period indicate the volume a... pular Science; 10-11, International Review; 23, Century; 27-8, ... tion; 47-8, Atlantic; 62-4, Harper; 97, Eclectic; 149-51, Living Ag...

left of the period indicate the volume as follows: 1-9, 20-21, Popular , International Review; 23, Century; 27-8, Lippincott's; 31-3, Nation; ; 62-4, Harper; 97, Eclectic; 149-51, Living age.

Tours, 61.385*
Towle, G. M., 33,456
Town, model suburban, 62.-481a*
Townsend, *G: A.*, 32.226; *L. T.*, 32.49
Trade, "travelers," 28.420; *U. S.* foreign, 11.566a; 33.-444; (Brazil) 33.471
Trades, instruction, 23.285a; Unions, (Eng.) 33.269
Transvaal, 32.3, 28, 69, 105, 143, 161, 215, 236; 33.45, 65, 85, 283, 285, 305, 327, 345; 150.424*,*a; 151.163*,*a
Trautz, G., 31.410
Traveling, w, 31.428
Treasury, U. S., 33.346, 406: frauds, 33.366
Trees, age, 3.321a*
Trelawny, E: J: 151.486a
Tremain, gen., 33.468
Trevelyan, 27.109||
Trier, bp. of, 33.187
Trinidad, 151.701
Tripoli & France, 33.25, 85
Troglodytes, 2.699a¶
Troitzkoi legend, 64.105
Trollope, A., 28.527; 32.172; 33.75||, 257
Troy, site, 32.166, 219, 315a; 33.451a; 150.771a; w, 32.-96a
Trumbull, *w**, 33.254; L., q, 33.206
Tuckey, J.. 31.278||
Tufts, W. W., q. 33.293
Tunis, history, 150.308a; French in, 32.253, 289, 309, 311a, 343, 363a; 33.45, 46a, 63, 65, 70a, 85, 107, 185, 187, 209, 227, 228a, 245, 265; 33.-262, 285, 305, 327, 347, 366, 387, 407, 427, 445, 465, 474, 483, 485; 150.349; and England, 32.402a
TURGENIEV, 97.440; 150.-692a
Turkey [see Mohammedanism], w, 32.338; *travels* med., 32.211a; *finance*, 31.-335; 33.327, 347, 425; *forein relations*, Austria, 150.349; *history*, w, 33.240; cont., 31.247, 265, 281, 320a, 387; 33.407; 61.745a; attentats, 33.167; murders, 31.335; *post-office*, 33.445; *society*, 62.603a
Turner, *w**, 32.8; C: T., 32.8
Turpin, 32 408
Tuson, R: V., 15.129
Twain, 40.843
Twins, 8.345a
Tyfoid, 14.514a; 16.460a
Tyler, K. E., 28.632; 33.455; *M. C.*, 33.373
Tylor, E. B., 33.181
Tyndall, 1.751; 2.103a*; 6.-500; *w*, 8.489; 11.63; fund, 32.316
Tyner, 33.301, 324, 326, 336
Type-writer, 23.155
Typografy, 33.174
Underwood, A. B. 32.32
Undset, I. 32.93
Union League decoration, 32.169;—Pacific monopoly, 33.113
Universal ins. co., 33.44
Universities, *U. S.* 33.173; 61.-253a; 62.627; comp. attendance, 3.235a; degrees, 32.-132; finance, 33.2; [endowments,] 11.258a; [expenses] 8.243a; govt. (self) 10.-510a; 19.555, 697; graduates (clergymen,) 11.114a; studies, evo., 16.556a; oratory, 6.622; science, 7.-402a; 9.467a; ps 10.313a;

17.693; *national*, 3.689; *German*, 31.302a; 61.253; 151.749a; professors, 33.-410; socialists, 48.801a

Upton, G: P. 32.118

Vaccination, 16.330a; 151.-329a

Vachot, *w*, 33.375§§

Vail, H: F., 33.245

Van Buren, T: B. 33.514

Vance, W. J. 47.714‡

Vanderbilt univ., 18.492; 14.-237; C. 32.335; W: H., 33.-130

Vane, sir H. 11.587a

Van Schaick, 33.64

Van Wyck, q, 33.224

Vassar, M. 33.128

Vaughan, D, 15.127, 556

Vedder, E. 32.150

Vega, see Carpio

Vegetables, 28.281a

Venice, 33.367; 151.635a; med. 151.312a; st. Marks, 31.321

Vennor, H: G. 32.12, 316, 350; 32.317, 473a

Ventilation, 1.356a; 7.596a; ps 11.196a¶; 18.577; 12.37a, 216a; 19.531; nht. air, 13.-105; hart disease, 2.183a

Venus, transit, 32.373; of Melos, 23.94a*; 33.333; w, 32.14a

Vergilius, *w*, 32.391¶; 149.-648

Vermont taxation, 33.44, 66a

Verne, 31.469‖; 32.17, 173; 33.361

Vernon T: 33.197**

Verrue, mrs de, 32.182a

Vessels, anc., 19.80a

Vetch, S., 11.462a

Victoria, hist., 33.25

Victoria, 61.221a*; husband, w, 31.365

Vienna, 32.237a; theatre fire, 33.465, 485, 505

Village communities, w, 32.-223, 260; 33.375, 492

Villari, *w*, 32.352

Villars, *w***, 32.368

Vincent, C. E. H. q, 33.88a; F, 63.794; *w*, 28.632; 33.-455; 48.837; H: 61.203*

Violins, 62.233a*

Viollet le Duc, 31.431

Virchow, q, 33.445; *w*, 14.-266a, 320a; 33.175

Virginia, (S. W.) w, 33.78; *finance*, 32.3, 68; 33.103, 106; *history*, early, w, 33.-93; records, 33.492; cont., 31.298, 322a, 334, 421; 32.-218, 239, 379, 398; 33.125, 128, 166, 225, 264, 304, 326, 383, 426, 464, 485; *society*, 20.271; 23.107; w, 32.248a; *sport*, 23.529a; *univ.* 33.-454

Vischer, R: 31.328

Vision, [see Eyes] 16.785a

Visions, [see Dreams] 17.-86a; 19.519a

Vivisection, 4.672a; 8.751; ps 10.363; 17.711; 19.409

Vizetelly, 32.139

VOGT, C. 13.20**a¶

Voice, 9.385a¶

Voltaire, 48.260a; youth, 47.-507a; w, 33.276a; 97.474a

Voorhees, q, 33.481

Wagner, P. 33.376†; *R:*, 33.217§§, 234§§, 317; w, 31.330

Waitz, 33.135

Waldo, q, 32.332

Waldstein, C: q, 32.75

Wales, women, 27.143a;

Figures to the left of the period indicate the volume as follows: 1-9, 12-20, Popular Science; 10-11, International Review; 23, Century; 27-8, Lippincott's; 31-3, Nation; 47-8, Atlantic; 62-4, Harper; 97, Eclectic; 149-51, Living Age.

Charlotte of, (marriage,) 150.377
Walker, F. A. 33.323; *J. B.* 33.258**
Walking, see Locomotion
Wallace, A. R. ps 11.235; *w* 32.47; 62.634; L, 33.209; *w*, 47.710‡; 62.152
Wallis, G: 14.336*
Walter, J: 63.845; q, 33.207, 324;
Walton, G: A. q, 61.934; I, 33.410; ed. 31.376
Wandering Jew, w, 32.221; 33.299
War, 2.457a; 32.4; 47.69
Ward museum, 8.460; F: T., 11.520; G., w, 33.517; H: A., 16.612; *T: H.*, 32.209a; 48.273a
Waring, G: W., q, 32.297; 33.304
Warner. C. D., 33.458‖, 498‖; *S.*, 33.336
Warren, gen., 33.63, 84; *F. E.* 33.19
Washington, w. 33.74; *helthfulnes*, 33.366, 386, 406, 445; *library*, 31.460a; *society*, history, 47.iii; 62.541a*; etiquet, 62.626
Washington and Lee univ. 33.134,
Washington territory, woman suffrage, 33.366
Water, 48.691a; drinking, 14.47a; fuel, 16.654a; odors, ps 11.469a; tales, 150.809, etc
Water color exh., N. Y. 32.80
Waterloo, 47.785a
Watson, J. C., 19.693*; 31.398; S., q, 32.240
Weather service, U. S., 16.289a; 31.389a; 33.366; w. 33.335
Weaver, 31.245; q, 31.451
Weber, w, 33.139
Webb, R: q, 33.293; *T. W.*, 33.453
Webster, *A.*, 33.477; D., 47.539
Weed, q, 33.404
Weeks, R. K., 32.319
*Weir, J. A.,** 32.250
Weisse, J. A., 14.678
Welbeck, 151.758
Welch lan., 33.192
Welles, J. H. 33.387
Wells, 16.71a, 397a
Werner, F. von, 33.413
Wesley, 11.320a
West, L. S., 33.305, 366
West, territories, surveys, 33.198, 512; travels, 61.185; sport, 151.535a
Wescott, B. F., 63.950
Western Union tel., 32.20, 35, 142; 33.64
Westminster abbey, 150.504
West Point, 31.349, 370; 32.2, 36, 58; 33.226, 484
West Virginia, travels, 61.ii*
Whales, 15.237a
Wheat [see Breadstufs] culture, U. S., 63.572a
Wheatstone, C: 8.363
Wheeler. A. C., 33.315; *L. N.*, 20.279; 33.239; *W: A.*, 33.374
Wheildon, W. W., 31.417
Whewell, W: 7.105*
Whipple, E. P., 62.384*
White House, 33.304; mts., 63.ii*; w, 33.413; R: G., q 62.625; *w*, 28.214§, 31.275; 31.291§; 63.633§
Whitebait, 97.563a
Whitman, W., 33.476
Whitney, M. W., 31.254; W:

Figures to the left of the period indicate the volume as follows: 1.9, 12-20, Popular Science; 10-11, International Review; 23, Century; 27-8, Lippincott's; 31-3, Nation; 74-8 Atlantic; 62-4, Harper; 97, Eclectic; 149-51, Living Age.

D., 15.121*; *w*,32.407; 33.-275
Whitridge, F. W., 33.242
Whittaker case, 32.2
Whittier, 32.319; 33.330‖, 393; 47.855
Whymper, E., 32.133
Wickham, W: C., q, 33.166
Wilbrandt, A., 33.334
Wilde, O. 33.28; *w* 23.152; 28.-423; 32.15; 33.101; 63.793
Wilder, B. G., 32.278
Wilhelm I, 33.107
Wilhelmj, 62.815*
Willard, S: q, 32.260
Willem II, 61.198*
Willis, G: P., 61.787
Williams vs. Brieffy, 32.2; college, 63.538a*
Williamson. A., 31.347§
Will o' the wisp, 19.57a
Wilmington, Del., hist., 62.-178a*
Wilson, A., 149.751; 150.383; J: 62.18*; *w*, 31.295;. J. F., 32.397; mrs. I. L., 33.-285
Wiltz, 33.305
Winchell, A., 13.492; 14.238
Windhorst, 33.465
Windmills, 18.217a
Windom. 32.159, 177; 33.264, 304, 326; q 32.160; 33.44, 346
Wines, French, price, 32.399; 33.82; 33.308a
Winsor, J., 23.153; 31.378; 32.265
Wisconsin, hist., 32.2; 33.244
Wis. Hist. Soc., 33.434
Wise, P., 33.245*
Wissenschaftliche Wochenblatter. 33.376
Wister, 33.276¶
Wöhler, F., 17.539a
Wolfe, C: S., 33.205, 282, 383, 403
Wolseley, 33.445
Woltmann. 31.427; 47.112
Women, [see Sex] 4.30a; q, 6.292; 14.201a; at 50, 150.-820a; blonde, and vice, 47.-136; bribery, 63.946; composers, 27.625; and crime, 8.1a; education, 4.748; 17.-823a; 62.101a, 947; w, 32.-356, (and helth) 16.521a; (co-op.,) 6.365; (financial) 31.249a; 47.138a; [Boston bank, *q. v.*, 10.698; [Madrid—] ps 10.371; equa'ity, 2.552a; fysicians, 32.316; fysical history, 18.191a; fysiology, 15.145a; girls, 23.-147; married (law). 18.-643a; (husband's liability) 31.452; and politics, 1.82a; position, hist., ps 11.433a; prairie, 27.415; and professions, 6.454a; in society, 33.214a; *suffrage*, 31.317; 32.387a; agitation, U. S., 33.282; w, 33.177a; and family, 6.87a
Wood college, 33.505; F., 32.-105; W: P., see Hatherley
Woodhull, V., 33.65
Woolf, 31.255
Woolsey, q, 33.22
Worcester, Mass. Ins., 23.-285; *dictionary*, 32.184
Wordsworth, 47.520; 62.26*, 171*, 342*; *w*, 32.153a
Worms, 151.433a
Worry, 151.229
Worsane, 33.380
Wright, H. B., 33.186
Writing, hand, 16.795a; 19.-620a
Wurtz, 32.284

Figures to the left of the period indicate the volume as follows: 1.9, 12-20, Popular Science; 10-11, International Review; 23, Century; 27.8, Lippincott's; 31-3, Nation; 47.8, Atlantic; 62-4, Harper; 97, Eclectic; 149-51, Living Age.

Wylde, see Wilde.
Wylie, J. A., 31.314
Wyman, J., 6.355*; 63.-672*; *T: B.*, 32.156
Yacht races, 33.265, 304, 387
Yale college, 17.265; 33.72a; finance, 33.2; N. Y. jubilee 33.431, 450; numismatics, w, 31.260; study, 33.49
Yates, E: 63.847*
Yeast, 1.578a
Yellow day, 33.208
Yonge, C. M. 32.178
Yorktown campaign, 33.-306a, 317; 63.323a*; w, 33.-295a; cel., 20.269; 33.264, 281, 284, 304, 323, 326, 346, 347, 386; 64.143
Young, C. A., 19.840a
Yvoire, 151.380
Zittell, 31.427
Zola, q, 33.316; *w*, 10.-144a; 31.382¶; 32.406; 33.-134; 47.116
Zollner, J. C. F. 48.417
Zulus, 10.564a; 33.435

ADDENDA.

Agassiz, 4.494, 608a*; and evo., 3.692a
Airy, sir G. B., 3.101a*
Alabama case: see, also, Ecl. & Living Age and Nation Indexes
Alchemy, 4.602a
Alcohol, 1·219a; 8.103a
Alps: see Ecl. and L. Age Index
America, climate, 1.665a; *U. S., finance*, Rev., 33.491; bonds, 33.482; *forein relations*, 33.502; *literature*, [see also Nation Index] *politics*, 17.557
Animals: see also Ecl. and L. Age Index
Apes, 7.665a
Apoplexy, 6.705a
Appletons' cyclop., 33.512
Architecture: see, also, Ecl. & L. Age Index
Arctic exploration [see Jeannette: also, Ecl. & Living Age Index], 7.320a, 468a
Art, see, also, Ecl. & Living Age, International, Nation. Lippincott, and Scribner Indexes]
Asfalt, 2.609a
Australia: see, also, Ecl. and L. Age Index
Babies, sci. considered, 97.-44a; and language, 9.129a¶
Bain, A. 9.360*
Bastian, H: C. 8.108
Baths, see, also, Ecl. & L. Age Index
Bats, 7.641a*; 9.523a*
Bears, 6.281a*
Beauty, see, also, Ecl. & L. Age Index
Bible [see, also, Ecl. & L. Age, International and Nation Indexes] soc., U. S. 33.504
Birds, [see, also, Ecl. & L. Age and Scribner Indexes] migration, 7.183a; U. S. 9.343a
Black deth in N. E., 3.28a
Blindness: see, also, Ecl. & L. Age Index
Bonapartes, see, also, Ecl. & L. Age, Lippincott and Scribner Indexes
Books, see, also, Ecl. & L. Age and Lippincott Indexes
Booth's Theater, 33.506

Boston, see, also, Lippincott and Nation Indexes
Brain, see, also, Ecl. & L. Age Index
Buddism, see, also, Ecl. & L. Age Index
Burial: see, also, Ecl. & L. Age and Lippincott Indexes
Burns: see Ecl. & L. Age Index
Byron, see Ecl. & L. Age Index
Calmucks, 1.419a*
Canada, see also, Ecl. and L. Age Index
Carlyle, see, also, Ecl. & L. Age Index
Cary, R. N. 33.257
Catholic church, see also, Ecl. & L. Age and Nation Indexes
Ceylon, see, also, Ecl. & L. Age Index
Chameleons, 6.526a*
Children (see, also, Ecl. & L. Age and Scribner Indexes) on stage, 33.507
China: see, also, Ecl. & L. Age and Nation Indexes
Chipmunks, 7.433a*
Christian church and religion: see, also, Ecl. & L. Age, Nation, and Scribner Indexes
Churchill, gov. 33.504
Civil service, English, 31.-247
Civilization, 1.603a; 7.195a, 332a
Cocoa tree, 2.214a
Coffin, J. H: 3.503a*
Coins, see, also, Ecl. & L. Age Index
Constantinople: see, also, Ecl. & L. Age Index
Conversation: see, also, Ecl. & L. Age Index
Co-operation: see, also, Nation Index.
Corundum 4.452a
Corpulence, see Obesity.
Dana, J. D., 1.362*
Darwin, 2.497*
Death, [see, also, Ecl. & L. Age Index] 3.270a¶
Delusions, [see Visions] 2.15a
Denmark: see, also, Ecl. and L. Age Index.
Diplomacy: see, also, Ecl. and L. Age Index.
Disease and mind, 8.177a
Divorce: see, also, Nation Index
Dogs: see, also, Ecl. and L. Age Index
Dress, [see, also, Ecl. and L. Age Index] history, 240a
Dyspepsia, [see Indigestion] 1.75a
Ears, 8.139a
Easterns: see Ecl. and L. Age Index
Education, [see, also, Ecl. & L. Age, International, Nation and Scribner Indexes] 1.129a, 496; classical, 1.-707a; sci., 1.624; 2.695; 3.-639a
Emotions, 1.274a; 2.434a*
England, [see, also, Nation Index] *admin.*, army, 2.-461a; *schools*, public, 2.-671a
English language [see, also, Nation and Lippincott Indexes].

Figures to the left of the period indicate the volume as follows: 1-9, 12-20, Popular Science; 10-11, International Review; 23, Century; 27-8, Lippincott's; 31-3, Nation; 47-8, Atlantic; 62-4, Harper; 97, Eclectic; 149-51, Living age.

Evidence: see, also, Nation Index
Evolution, 1.313a; 2.110a; 4.-713a
Fever, 28.104
Fiction: see, also, Ecl. & L. Age and Nation Indexes.
Filosofy: see, also, Ecl. & L. Age and International Indexes
Florence: see, also, Ecl. and L. Age Index
Flowers: see, also, Ecl. and L. Age Index
Folklore: see, also, Ecl. & L. Age, Nation and Lippincott Indexes
Food: see, also, Ecl. and L. Age Index
Fotografy: see, also, Ecl. and L. Age Index
Furniture: see, also, Scribner Index
Ghosts: see also Ecl. and L. Age Index
Glass: see also Ecl. & L. Age Index
Goethe, w, 48.688a
Gray, A. 1.491a*
Hair: see, also, Ecl. & L. Age Index
Hannibal & St. Jo. ry., 33.-208, 210
Horvard univ.: see, also, Nation Index
History: see, also, Ecl. & L. Age Index
Horses: see, also, Ecl. & L. Age Index
Household: see, also, Ecl. & L. Age, Nation, and Scribners Indexes
Hymnology: see, also, Ecl. & L. Age Index
Huguenots: see also, Nation Index
Hygiene: see also, Ecl. & L. Age and Lippincott Indexes
India: see also, Ecl. & L. Age, and Nation Indexes
Indians, U. S. see also, Nation Index
Insanity: see also, Ecl. & L. Age Index
Institutions: see also, Nation Index
Insurance: see, also, Nation Index
Japan: see, also, Ecl. & L. Age and Nation Indexes
Jews: see, also, Ecl. & L. Age and Nation Indexes
Knowledge: see, also, Ecl. and L. Age Index
Labor: see, also, Nation Index
Law: see, also, Ecl. & L. Age, International and Nation Indexes
Libraries: see, also, Nation Index
Life: see, also, Ecl. & L. Age Index
Literature: see, also, Ecl. & L. Age, Nation and Scribner Indexes
London: see, also, Ecl. & L. Age and Lippincott Indexes
Man: see. also, Ecl. & L. Age Index
Marriage: see, also. Ecl. & L. Age and Nation Indexes
Medical prof.: see, also. Nation Index
Mind: see, also, Ecl. & L. Age Index
Money: see, also, Ecl. & L.

Figures to the left of the period indicate the volume as follows: 1-9, 12-20, Popular Science; 10-11, International Review; 23, Century; 27-8, Lippincott's; 31-3, Nation; 47-8 Atlantic; 62-4, Harper; 97, Eclectic; 149-51, Living Age.

Age, International and Nation Indexes
Morals: see, also, Ecl. & L. Age and Nation Indexes
Music: see, also, Ecl. & L. Age, Lippincott and Nation Indexes
Mythology: see, also, Ecl. & L. Age Iudex
Nature: see, also, Ecl. & L. Age Index
New York: see, also, Nation and Scribner Indexes
New Zealand: see, also, Ecl. & L. Age Index
Orientals: see, also, Easterns
Paris: see, also, Ecl. & L. Age, Lippincott, Nation and Scribner Indexes
Philadelphia: see, also, Lippincott Index
Plants: see, also, Ecl. & L. Age and Scribner Indexes
Political Economy: see, also, International Index
Politics: see, also, Ecl. & L. Age and Nation Indexes
Prisons: see, also, Nation Index
Punishment: see,also, Nation Index
Quakers: see, also, Ecl. & L. Age Index
Railways: see, also Nation and Scribner Indexes
Reading: see, also, Scribner Index
Religion: see also, Ecl. & L. Age Index
Rome: see, also, Ecl. & L. Age and Lippincott Indexes
Science: see, also, Ecl. & L. Age, International and Nation Indexes
Shakspere: see, also, Lippincott and Nation Indexes
Silver question: see also, International Index
Stage, see, also, Ecl. & L. Age, Lippincott and Scribner Indexes
Taxation: see, also, Nation Index
Trade: see, also, Ecl. & L. Age and Nation Indexes
War: see, also, Internationa Index
Women: see, also, Ecl. & L. Age, Nation, and Scribner Indexes

Figures to the left of the period indicate the volume as follows: 1-9, 12-20, Popula Science; 10-11, International Review; 23, Century; 27-8, Lippincott's; 31-3, Nation; 47-8 Atlantic; 62-4, Harper; 97, Eclectic; 149-51, Living Age.

The compiler gratefully acknowledges the courtesy of the publishers of the following periodicals in exchanging with the ANNUAL INDEX, and thereby greatly facilitating the labor of preparing the second year's issue.

Atlantic, Magazine of Art, Century, Deutsche Rundschau, Eclectic, Harper's, International, Lippincott's, Living Age, Nation, New Englander, North American, Penn, Potter's.

The publishers of the Canadian Monthly, Catholic World, Popular Science, and Princeton Review have not seen fit thus to cooperate in the enterprise.

Q. P. Index has done and is doing very notable work in making indexes to current periodicals. It is easy to underestimate the service of a good index, but the student of recent literature will find the indexes already published by Q. P. Index, both valuable and reliable.—*N. Y. Times*, 9, 1, 1882.

A great work for readers and students, in enabling them to refer, at a minimum expenditure of time and trouble, to multiform and extensive sources of information on almost every conceivable topic, has been accomplished in the preparation of the so-called "Q. P. Indexes" to a number of our most important periodicals—Scribner's ($2), the Atlantic Monthly, ($1.25), the International Review, ($1), Lippincott's Magazine, ($2), the Nation, ($2.50), the Eclectic and Littell's Living Age ($3). By an ingenious though simple system of abbreviation and contraction, the contents of each of these publications for a long series of years is so summarized in small space that it takes but a moment to turn to everything that has been printed on any subject discussed in their pages. WE DO NOT SEE HOW THE WORK COULD BE BETTER DONE.—*Country Gentleman*, 18, 1, 1882.

[The Q. P. Indexes] will not be rendered superfluous by Mr. Poole's, because they go very much more into detail than an index covering so much ground as Mr. Poole's could possibly do, and because they give an alphabetical list of the authors of articles which Mr. Poole's index will not do. IT WILL BE A MISTAKE, therefore, for any library which wishes to encourage research NOT TO SECURE THE WHOLE SERIES OF THE Q. P. INDEXES.—*Library Journal*, March, 1881.

Your Living Age Index is indispensable.—*Rev. W. S. Bullard, Snowville, Va.*

You are doing a good work for every library or professional man who has for years accumulated any of the leading periodicals in anything like completeness. In my own case, you have not only removed all temptation to dispose of a large collection of periodicals to the second-hand dealers, because there was so much labor in making them available, but you have placed in my way the temptation to complete some sets to which I have been a subscriber for years.—*Rev. E. S. Frisbee, President Wells College.*

Q. P. Index Annual. 1881.

ur "Living Age" Index supplies a long-felt want. I have Age" from the commencement, and the index will save me nly much valuable time, but go far towards preserving a lly amiable temper.—*S. F. Seager, Lansing, Mich.*

[It will be observed that this list includes all the larger libraries except A bany st.te, y. m., Amherst college, Bowdoin college, Brooklyn, Columbia college, Hartford y. m., Newark ly. asso., Newport *People's*, N. Y. apprentices,' Society, Princeton college, Rochester, N. Y., Ath., San Francisco public.

The following libraries have bought one or more of the Q. P. INDEX publications. (***A***, *indicates* "*Atlantic*" ***Index*** ($1.25); ***E***, "*Eclectic and Living Age*" ($3.00); ***I***, "*International*" ($1.00); ***L***, "*Lippincott's*" ($2.00); ***N***, "*Nation*" ($2.-50); ***S***, "*Scribner's*" ($2.00); ***a***, *ANNUAL* ($1.00); ***m*** "***MONOGRAPH***," ($2.00).

College and School Libraries.

Bangor Theological Seminary,	*N*
Bates,	*A, E*
Beloit,	*N*
Brown,	*N*
California,	*N*
Cornell College,	*A, E, I, L, N, a*
" Univ.,	*N*
Dartmouth,	*A, E, I, L, N, m*
Hamilton	*A*
Harvard,	*A, E, I, L, N, S, m*
Haverford,	*A, E, I, N*
Iowa Univ.,	*A*
Johns Hopkins,	*A, E, I, L, N, S, a, m*
Lafayette,	*N*
Lehigh,	*N*
Madison,	*m*
Marietta,	*E. N*
Michigan agric. college,	*A, E, S,*
" univ.	*N*
New York City,	*A, E, I*
Northwestern,	*N*
Oberlin,	*N*
Ohio,	*A, N*
Olivet,	*A, E, I, N*
Rochester,	*N*
Rutgers,	*N*

St. Cloud, Minn., Normal, *m*
Swarthmore, *A, E, L, N, m*
Union, *N*
Vassar, *A*
Vermont, *A, E, I, N, S*
Wabash, *E, I, m*
Wellesley, *A*
Wells, *A, E, N, S*
Western Maryland, *E, m*
Williams, *N*
Yale, *E, N*

Free and Chartered Libraries.

Alameda, Cal. [public] *A*
Auburn, N. Y., [Seymour] *A, E*
Baltimore, [Peabody] *A, N*
Bloomington, Ill., [ly. asso.] *A*
Boston, [Athenæum], *A, E, I, L. N, S, m*
" [public], *A, E, I, L, N, S*
" [Fellowes Athenæum] *I*
Braintree, Mass., [public], *A*
Bridgewater, Mass., [public], *E, S*
Bristol, R. I., [public] *A*
Brockton, Mass., [public], *A*
Brooklyn, [Hist. Soc.], *N*
Buffalo, [Y. M. Asso.], *A. E. I, L, S*
Burlington, [Fletcher], *A, E, I, L, N, m*
Carson City [state] *m*
Chicago, [public], *E, N*
Chicopee, Mass., [public], *A*
Cincinnati, [mer.] *A, E. N*
" [public] *A, E, I, L, N, S, m*
Cleveland, (public), *A, E*
" (Case), *A, E, L, N, S, a*
Clinton, Mass., (public), *A, E, S*
Dayton, O., (public), *A, E, L, N*
Desmoines, (public), *A*
" (state), *I*
Fall River, (public), *A, E, I, L, N, S*
Fitchburg, Mass., (public), *A*
Framingham, Mass.,(public,) *A*
Fremont, Ohio, (Birchard), *A, E, m*
Germantown, Pa., (Friends), *N*
Harrisburg, (state), *A, E, L, N, S*
Haverhill, (public), *A, L, N, m*
Hingham, Mass., (public), *A*
Holyoke, Mass., (public), *A*
Indianapolis, (public), *A, E, I, L, N, S, a*
Ithaca, (Cornell). *A*
Lansing, [state], *A, E, I, L, N, m*
Lawrence, Mass., [public] *A, L*
Lenox, Mass., (ly. asso.), *A*
Lowell, (public), *A, E, L, S*
Lynn, (public), *A, m*
Madison, Wis., (Hist. Soc.] *A, E, I, L, N, m*
" " (public), *A, N,*
Manchester, N. H., (City), *A*
Melrose, Mass., (public), *A*
Middletown, Conn., (Russell), *A*
Milwaukee, (public), *A, E, I, L, N, S, a, m*
Minneapolis, (Athenæum) *A*

New Bedford, (public), *A, E, I, N, m*
Newburyport, (public), *A*
Newport, (Redwood), *N*
Newton, Mass., (public), *A*
New York, [Astor], *E, N*
" [Mercantile], *A, I, L*
" [Y. M. C. A.] *E, I, N*
" [Cooper Union], *A, E, I*
" [Century Club], *A, N*
Pawtucket, [public], *A, E, L, N, m, S*
Peoria, [Mercantile], *A*
Philadelphia, [Library Co.], *A, E, I, L, N, S*
" [Mercantile], *A, I, L, N*
" [Mutual,] *m*
Pittsburg, [ly. asso.], *A, E, I, L, N*
Portland, [public] *A, E, I, L, N, S*
Providence, [public], *A, E, N, S*
" [Athenæum], *A, E, I, N, S*
Quincy, Mass., *A, E,*
St. Louis, [public schools], *A, E, I, L, N*
" [Mercantile] *A*
St. Paul [Library], *A, S*
San Francisco, [Mercantile], *A, E, I, L, N*
" [Odd Fellows'], *A, E, N, m*
Somerville, Mass., [public], *A*
Southbridge, Mass., *A.*
Springfield, Mass., [City], *A, E, I, N, m*
Stockbridge, Mass., [Jackson], *A, E, S*
Syracuse, N. Y., [Central], *A, m*
Taunton, Mass., [public], *A, E, I, L, N, S*
Topeka, [state], *E,*
Warren, Mass., [ly. asso.], *A. S.*
Washington, [Congressional], *E, N*
" [Bureau of Education] *I*
Waterbury, Conn., [Bronson], *A, N*
Westfield, Mass., [Athenæum], *A*
West Winstead, Conn., [Beardsley], *A, I, S*
Wilmington, Del., [Athenæum], *N*
Woonsocket, [Harris], *A*
Worcester, Mass., [pub.] *A, E, I, L, N, S, a, m*

rice's marriage, death, Dante's public life, 3, 4, 5, 6; marriage, relations to wife, 3; exile, 5; wanderings, 6, 7; death, 7.

Darmstadt, landgrafin Caroline of, IV, 8.

DASHKOV, princess, unpopularity in old age undeserved VIII, 1; birth, education, 2; marriage, revolutionary intrigues, 3; rewards, widowhood and poverty, energy and economy, travels, in Edinburgh, son's education, 5; becomes director of academy, reforms, 6; successful administration, persecuted by Paul, 7; exile, last years, 8.

England, *crown*, legitimate heir, II, 22; *history*: state in 1603, VI, 3; royal policy revolutionary, 3; revolution of 1641. 9, different views of, 8; compared with French, 1, 2, 4; superiority of English leaders, 2, 8; complete triumph of Puritan party, 1; moral enthusiasm the cause, 6; its successful statesmanship, 1, 2; connection with Continental Protestantism, 4; its fall, 2, 3; causes, 4, 11; how it might have been avoided, 5; effects of this, 11; revolution causes no social change, 4; military government greater evil than royal tyranny, 10; the Restoration salutary, 9, 11, [see STUART] 18th cent. politics, XXIV, 3.

ERASMUS, parentage, XVII, 1; youth, 2; studies, works, 3, 4; in Italy, 5; in England, 6; success, 6; position in the Reformation, 7, 8; his wit, 9; last years, 10.

Etrurians, character, XIII, 6.

Florence, mediæval, XV, 2, 4.

Fouquet, cause of his fame, XX, 1; patronage of intellect, 2; mansion, 2; power, 3, 6; confesses his jobs, 6; why hated by king, 6; grand fete, 7; arrest, 7; friends, 8; fate, 11.

FRANCE, ITS GROWTH AND CONSOLIDATION, I, 1; vague notions of French history, caused by ignorance of historical geography, 1; connection with Gaul, 2, 3; nature of its growth, 3; appearance of the Franks, 5; has no right to claim their conquests, 7; beginning of nation, 8; Paris its centre, 14; government in 987, 16; divisions, independence of vassals, possesses no seaport, 17; results expulsion of the English, 18; attracts eastern neighbors, 19; and southern, 20, [see IRON MASK, FOUQUET.] The revolution, its opposing principles, their vitality, VI, 1, 2; want of statesmanship in leaders, 2, 8; consists of two revolutions, XXII, 4; [see BONAPARTE] *society*, limited hospitality, IV, 6; under Louis XIV, XX, 1.

Freeman, E. A., I.

French language, IV, 7; literature, meretricious character, IV, 7.

Friedrich Barbarossa, significance of the legend, XXV, 1; origin, 4.

Geneva described, XV, 1; in 15th century, resistance to duke of Savoie, 2; under Calvin, 3;

German literature, "storm and stress" period, Wertherism, IV, 18; [see Weimar].

Germany, *constitution*, mediæval, XVIII, 1; cities, 2; *history*; league of cities, 3; political side of Reformation, 4; peasants' war [see HERDER, MOLTKE, ZINZENDORF].

Godkin, E. L., XXIV.

Goethe, IV, 9, 18, 27; criticised by Merck, 10; in Strassburg, 13; Weimar, 21; gets Herder there, 19.

Greeks, inferiority as politicians, XIII, 9.

Hale, E. E., XXVII.

Hansa, XVIII, 4.

Hayward, A., II, OII.

HERDER, early life, IV, 1; education, 3; character, 4, 28; social success, 5, 6; discontent, 5, 6, 15, 18, 27; in Riga, 5; works, 6, 17, 28; in France, 6, 8; tutor to prince, meets Miss Flachsland and Merck, 8; in Buckeburg, 11, 15, 17; religious fervor, 14, 15; opportunities to change profession, 15; intimacy with countess, 16; marriage, 17; in Weimar, 19, 23; eloquence, bad temper, 24; domestic happiness, 26; in Italy, 26; death, 28.

Hillebrand, K., IV.

History, opinions on, X, 12; literary, contrasted with scientific, VI, 7, 10; bad effects of former, VI, 7.

Hus, Johann, division of his followers, X, 1, see Moravians.
Hutten, U. von, XVIII, 5.
INDIA, enormous results achieved by E. I. Co., XXIV, 1, 2, 7; an outlet for the energy of the English middle class, 3, 4; early misgovernment and extortion, 5; immobility of the people, 6; inconsistency of policy, 8; hold on affections of English people, 9.
IRON MASK identified with count Matthioly, XIV, 1; popular version of the story makes him brother of Louis XIV, 2, 3; the Matthioly story, 3, 4, 5; proved false, 6, 7, 8; first knowledge of Iron Mask, 6; identified with the conspirator "L. Oldendorf," 9, 10; why not put to death, 10; intrinsic impropbability of conspirator version, 10, 11; possible motives for keeping, but not killing, the Mask, 11; his resemblance to the king, likelihood of his being his brother, substitution theory, 12.
Italy, [see Florence, Venice,] *history*, the imperial power, conflict with the church, XVI, 1, [see DANTE, ALFIERI].
KALB, JOHANN, birth, enters French army, XI, 1; services, marriage, visits America, becomes major-general U. S. A., 3; death, 4.
KIDD, Capt., commissioned to capture pirates, XXVII, 1; surrender, 3; trial, 5.
Kyfhausser, the, XXV, 1.
Lafayette, XI, 2, 3.
Lauzun, XX, 12.
Louis XIV, character, XX, 4; changes of fortune, 5.
Luther, political views, part in the Peasants' War, XVIII, 6; what he accomplished, 8.
Marriage in Egypt, V, 2; Rome, 3.
Matthioli, see Iron Mask.
Mazarin, XX, 3.
Merck, J: H:, IV, 8, 9, 10.
Mohammed II, IX, 5, 6.
MOLTKE, count: appearance, birth, school life, VII, 1; enters Prussian army, poverty, becomes captain, 2; life in Turkey, works, travels, marriage, life in Rome, 3; promotion Austrian war, 4.
MORAVIAN BRETHREN, origin, effect Wiclif's writings, settlements, bible translation, persecution X, 1; prosperity, emigration to Poland, abandoned at peace of Westphalen, clergy, 2; worldly amusements forbidden, marriage, foundation of Herrnhut, 3; school for noblemen, missions, 5, 6; regime at Herrnhut, school discipline, 7; dogma, 8.
Mountain, Old Man of, see Assassins.
Pocahontas, popular version of her story a myth, XIX, 5, 10-12.
Poland, *history*, interest felt in, XXIII, 1; mediæval privileges of nobility, wretched condition of people, 2; elections, parliamentary procedure, magnificence of nobles, 3-6; last struggle, 8; effect of partition, XXII, 5 *society*, house and dress, a ball, gaming, XXIII, 6-10; women, 13.
Political opinions, effect of literary skill upon, VI, 7.
Politics, effect of religion in, VI, 5, 11; origin of republic and monarchy XII, 9; the power that succeeds a revolution, XXII, 1; "imperialism" defined, 2.
Poniatovski, S., XXIII, 7.
Potocka, Felix and wife, XXIII, 11.12
Prussian army in 1760, IV, 3.
Puritanism, see England
Reformation, see Erasmus, Germany.
Riga in 18th century, IV, 5.
ROME, character of its greatness, not accounted for by race, due to intellectual superiorty, XIII, 1; a wealthy commercial city, 2, 3; its republican character, effect of conquests, 3; inferiority to hill tribes equalized by discipline, 4; civil and military government harmonized, 5; cause of its superiority as ruling power, accessibility to foreign ideas, 6; colonies, local self-govt, mingling of tribes, source of universal character of Roman law, 7; religion not absent from Roman life, 8; cause of the failure of the republic, XXII, 2; Roman marriage, V, 3.

INDEX.

Russia, revolution of 1762, VIII, 4, [see DASHKOV].

SCANDERBEG, fame, birth, IX, 1; education, military talent, deserts Turks, 2; recovers Albania, 3; struggles with Turks, 4, 5, 6; death, character, 7.

Scarron, carnival frolic, XX, 2.

Schaumburg-Lippe, count of, romantic career in Portugal, local reforms, IV, 12; character, 14; wife, 15; death, 19.

Schiller, character, IV, 27.

Seeley, J: R:, VI, 7; XXII.

Semites, character, XIII, 9.

SERVETUS, trial and execution, XXVI, 1-4.

SMITH, capt. J: adventurous career, XIX, 1; mendacious disposition, 3; not saved by Pocahontas, 10-12.

Shelton, F: W., XX.

Smith, Goldwin, XIII.

STUART, CHARLES EDWARD: birth, education, II, 1; his Scotch expedition, its brilliant character, not its leader, 3; his degradation, 2, 5,; contradictions of his career, character, 3; courage, popularity, 4; cause of retreat, returns to France, expulsion thence, 4; visits London, is summoned to Paris, reasons for marriage, 5; condition, 6; in Rome, 7; in Florence, 8, 15; behavior to his wife, 12; summons his daughter, 15; cures scrofula, death, 16; alleged descendants, 8.

Taylor, B., XXV.

Thuringen, XXV, 1.

United States, see America, U. S.

VENICE: romantic character of its history, III, 1; generally misrepresented, 1, 2; new material for, 2; the council of ten, mystery one of its weapons, 1; records, 2, 4; character of inquisition, 2; mild in its judgments, 3; power, 3; spies, 4; the prisons, use of poison, 7; diplomacy at Venice, 4; venality of nobles, 5; difficulty of keeping state secrets, Barbaro case, 5.

Washington, G: character, XI, 3.

War, how discipline equalizes weak with strong, XIII, 9.

Weil, G. XXI, 5.

Weimar the intellectual capital, IV, 19; duchess Anna-Amelia, group of authors stage, 20; Carl August's accession, 21; gay life, 21, 23; Goethe's importance, 23; Herder shocked, 25.

Werner, Z., IV, 4.

Wesley visits Herrnhut, X, 7; quarrels with Moravians, 8.

WHIST, 0II.

Wieland, IV, 20.

ZINZENDORF, COUNT, youth, becomes religious, X, 4; travels, 4, 9; marriage, 5; ordained preacher, exiled, 6; generosity, becomes bishop, 8; goes to St. Thomas, 9; humility, money troubles, 2d marriage, 10; works, death, 11.

Lightning Source UK Ltd.
Milton Keynes UK
UKHW021608110119
335365UK00008B/735/P

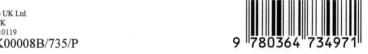

9 780364 734971